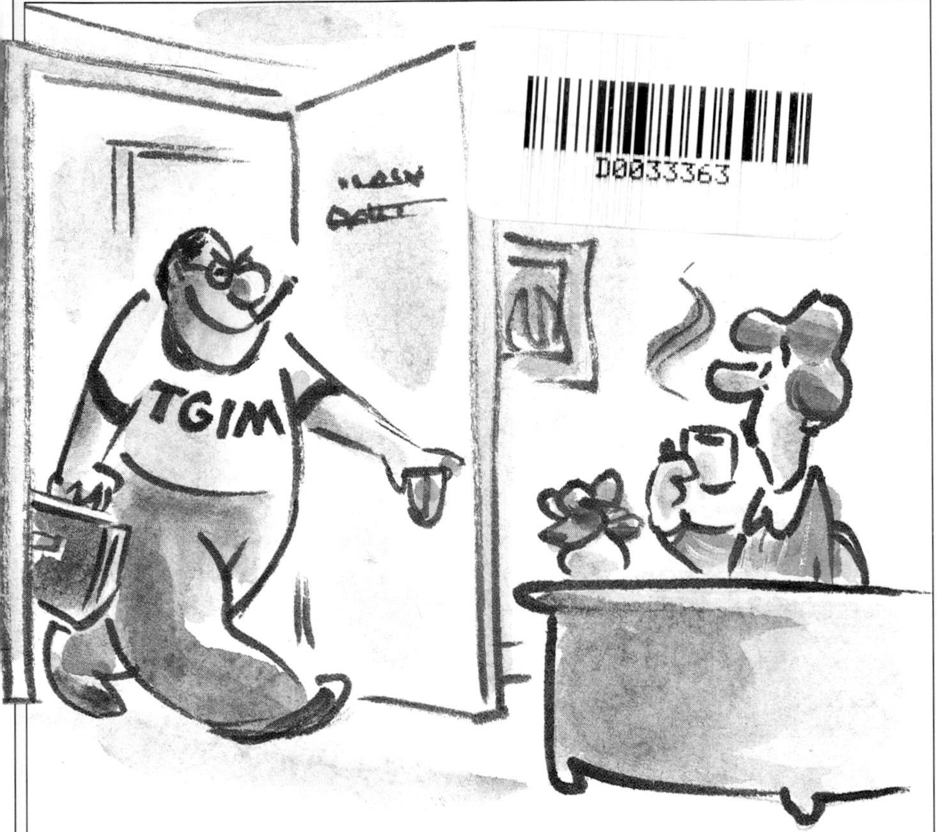
TGIM

You prefer Mondays to Fridays.

YOU KNOW YOU'RE A WORKAHOLIC WHEN...

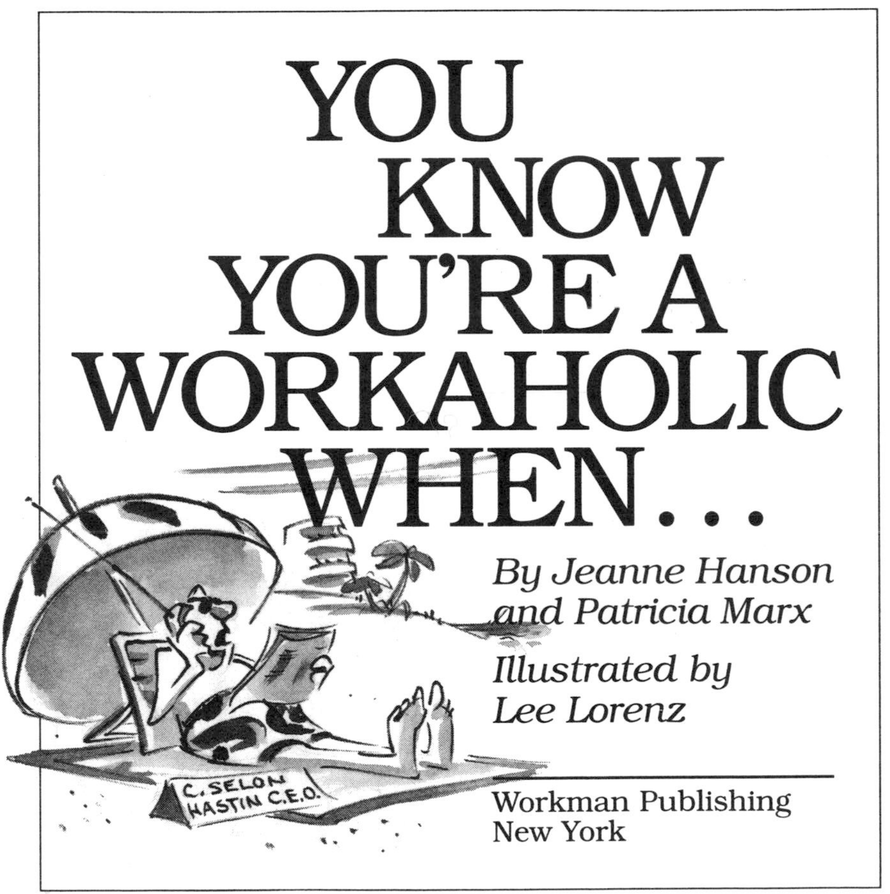
C. SELON
HASTIN C.E.O.

By Jeanne Hanson and Patricia Marx

Illustrated by Lee Lorenz

Workman Publishing
New York

Library of Congress Cataloging-in-Publication Data
Hanson, Jeanne K.
You know you're a workaholic when . . .
Jeanne K. Hanson, Lee Lorenz.   p. cm.

ISBN 1-56305-470-1 (pbk.)
1. Workaholics—Humor. 2. American wit and humor.
I. Lorenz, Lee. II. Title.

PN6231.W645H36 1993 818'.5402—dc20 92-50935
CIP

Workman books are available at special discounts when
purchased in bulk for premiums and sales promotions as well as
for fund-raising or educational use. Special editions or book excerpts can
also be created to specification. For details, contact the Special
Sales Director at the address below.

Workman Publishing
708 Broadway
New York, NY 10003
Manufactured in the United States

10 9 8 7 6 5 4 3 2 1

Workaholics are everywhere: wheeling and dealing in tower offices or hunched over their desks in backroom cubicles; busy behind the counter at the mom-and-pop store or all-night cleaner's (open 365 days a year); ensconced in suburban dens and basements, planning to open their own business or start a second career.

Some people think workaholics are crazy, but not us. All those men and women you see eating on the run as they hurry past you, rushing home after work to do even more, embody the Puritan ethic, the American dream, the immigrant push in all of us to get ahead. They're the ones who keep us moving, and without them our world would grind to a halt.

So here's to all the workaholics out there. We know who you are and we salute you!

You Know You're a Workaholic When. . .

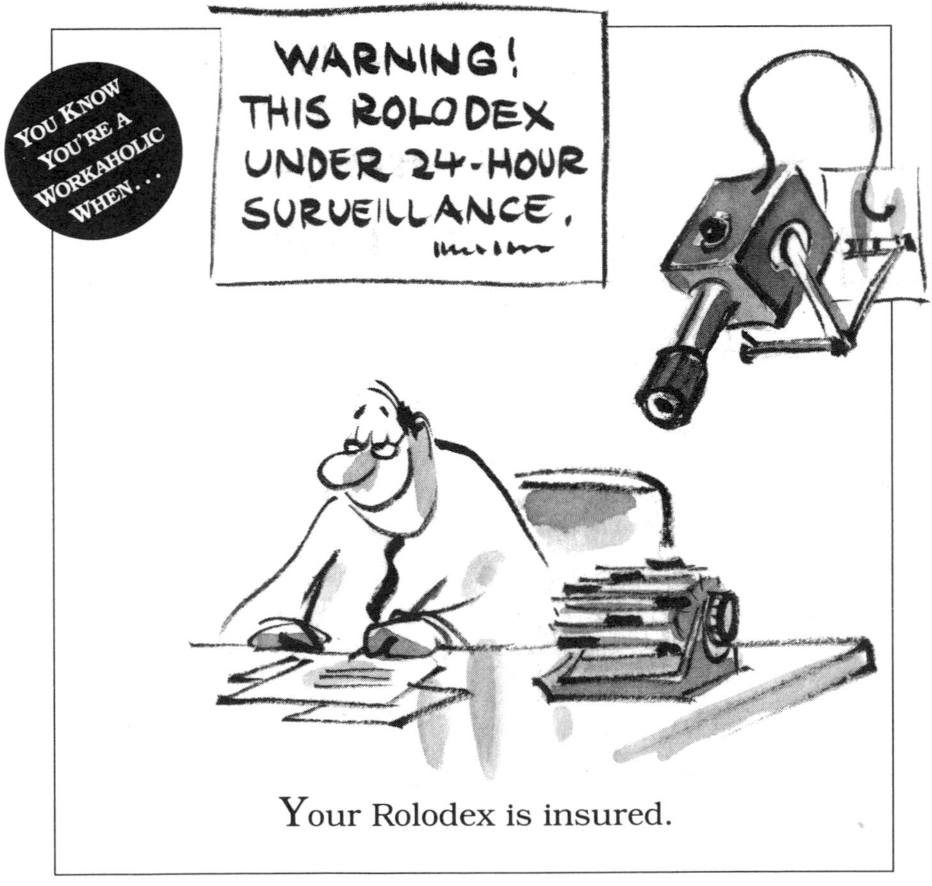
WARNING!
THIS ROLODEX
UNDER 24-HOUR
SURVEILLANCE.

Your Rolodex is insured.

You Know You're a Workaholic When . . .

You move to Australia to gain the extra day.

You wonder why anyone would buy the unabridged version of *War and Peace.*

You consider anyone who works a 9-to-5 day a retiree.

You never stop for refreshment.

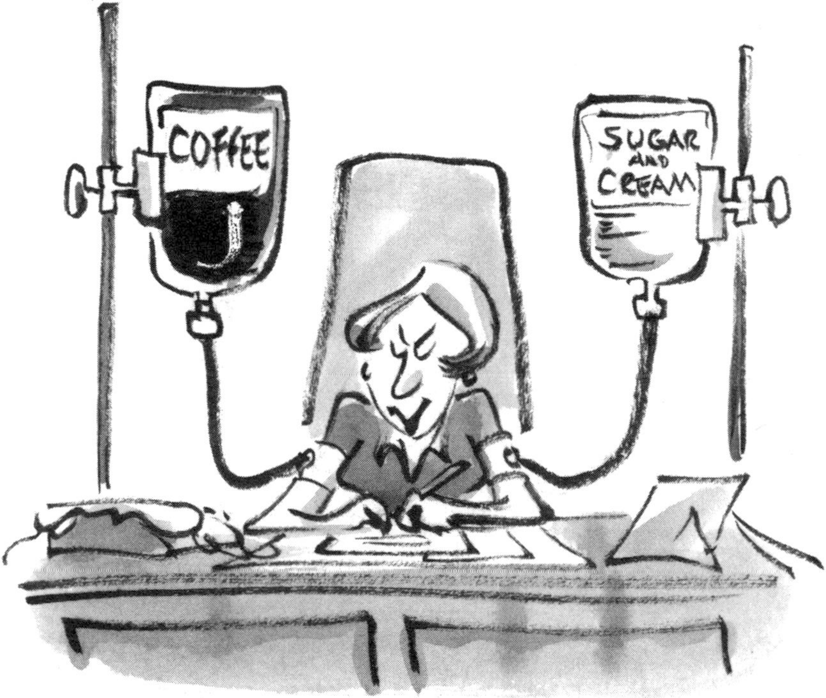
COFFEE
SUGAR AND CREAM

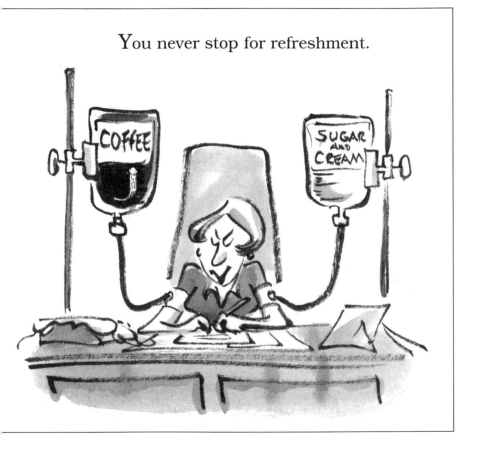

You Know You're a Workaholic When…

You hope that if you come back to
life as an animal,
it will be an octopus.

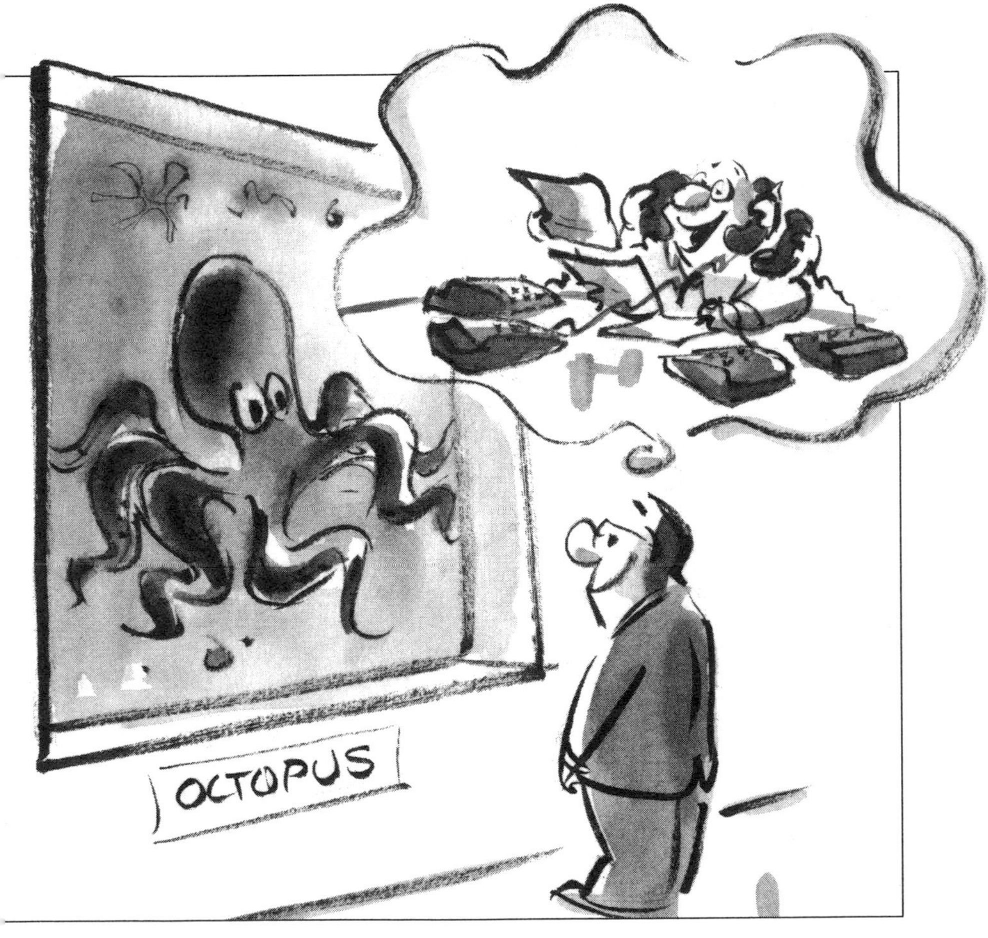
OCTOPUS

You Know You're a Workaholic When. . .

You can't believe it's time for your kid to have another birthday.

You decide to surprise your spouse by coming home early and discover your family went to Grandma's for the weekend.

You rent movies that you've already seen so you can work without watching.

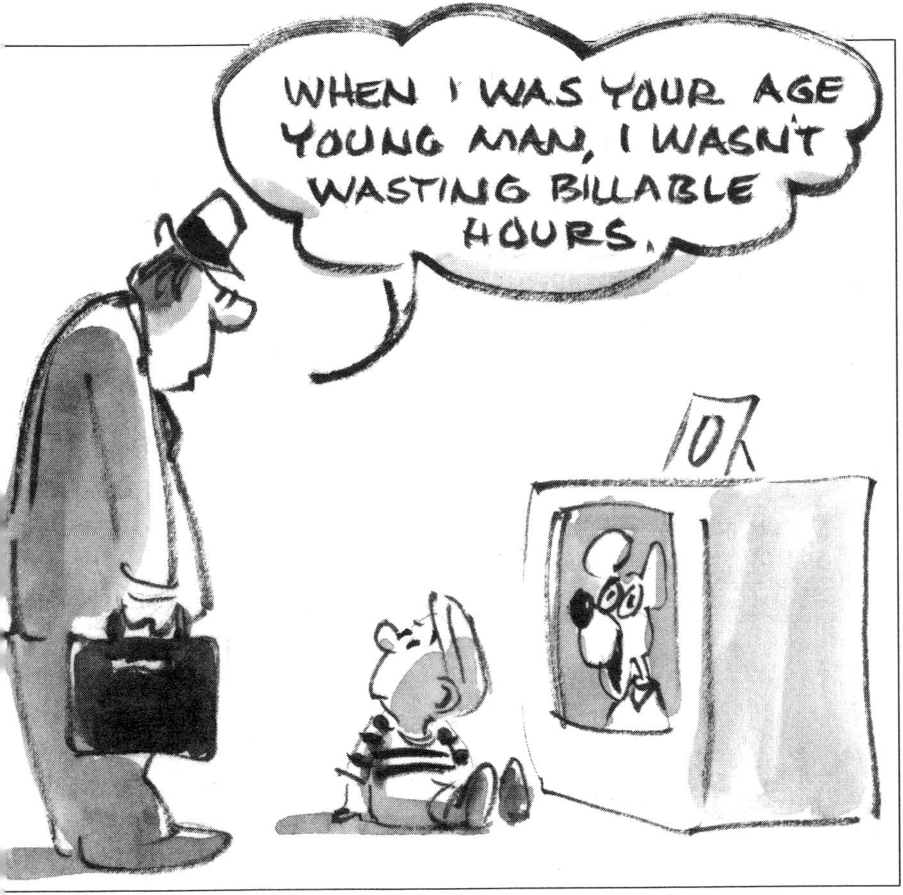
WHEN I WAS YOUR AGE YOUNG MAN, I WASN'T WASTING BILLABLE HOURS.

YOU KNOW YOU'RE A WORKAHOLIC WHEN...

You limit your trips to the bathroom to save time.

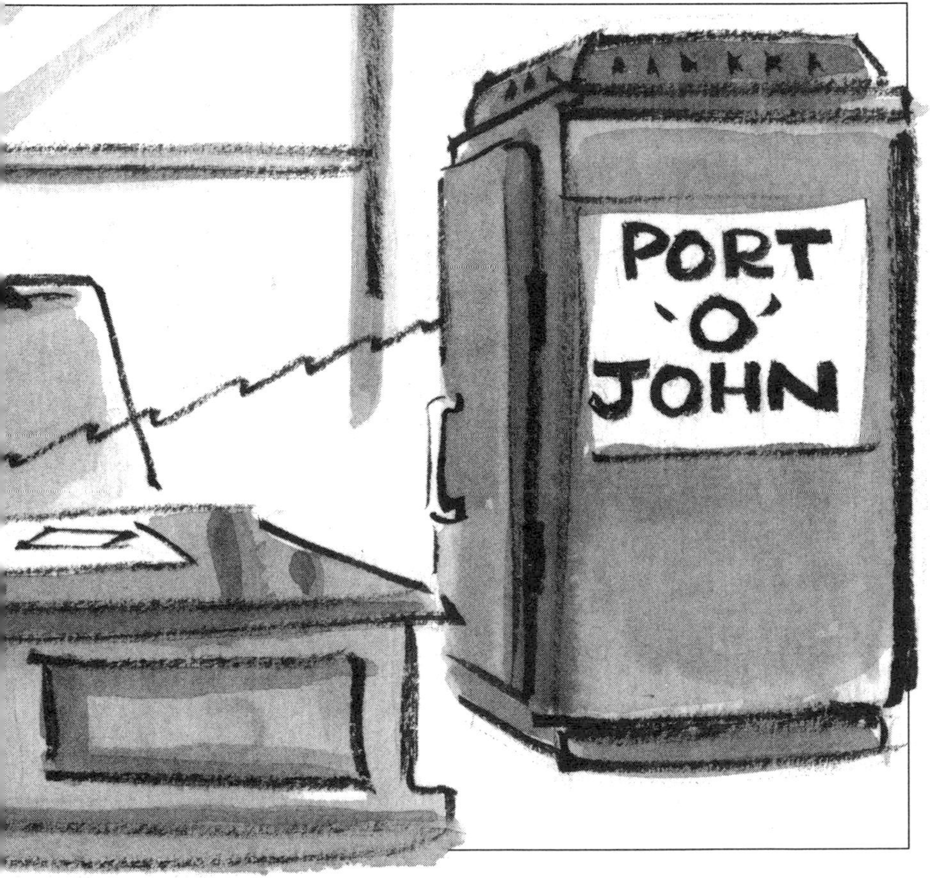
PORT
'O'
JOHN

YOU KNOW YOU'RE A WORKAHOLIC WHEN...

You write love letters on Post-its.

On the beach you hide your business report between the covers of *Travel and Leisure* magazine so your date thinks you're relaxing.

You take business cards to weddings.

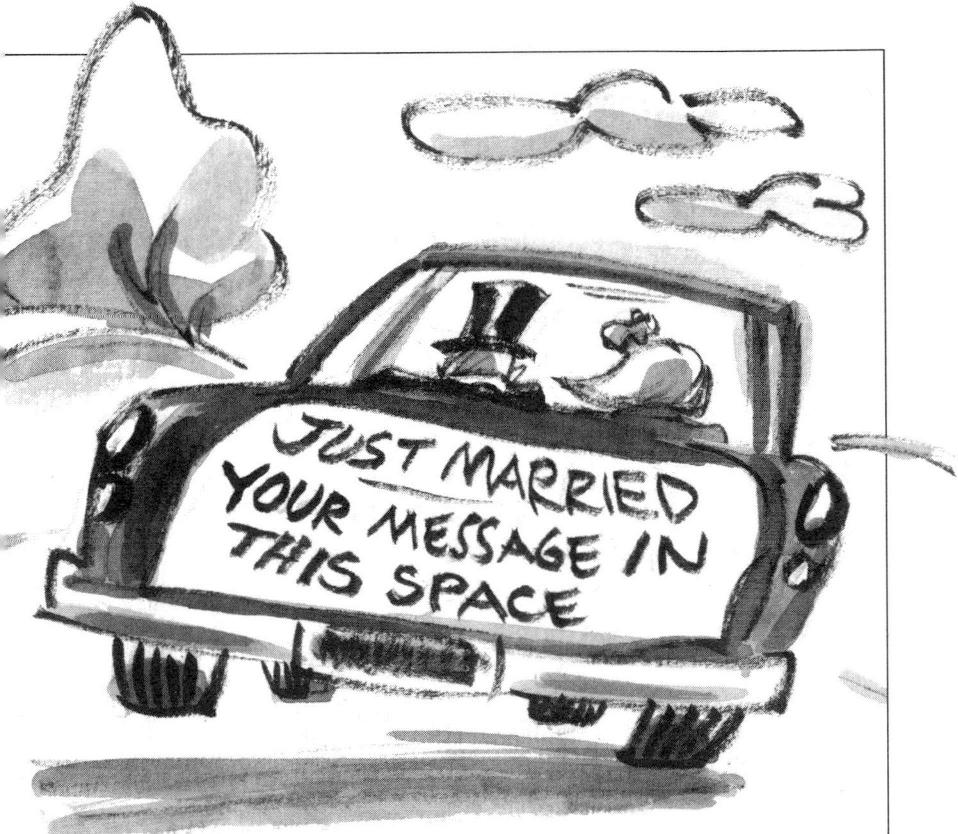
JUST MARRIED
YOUR MESSAGE IN
THIS SPACE

YOU KNOW YOU'RE A WORKAHOLIC WHEN. . .

You enjoy the music of John Cage because it reminds you of your beeper.

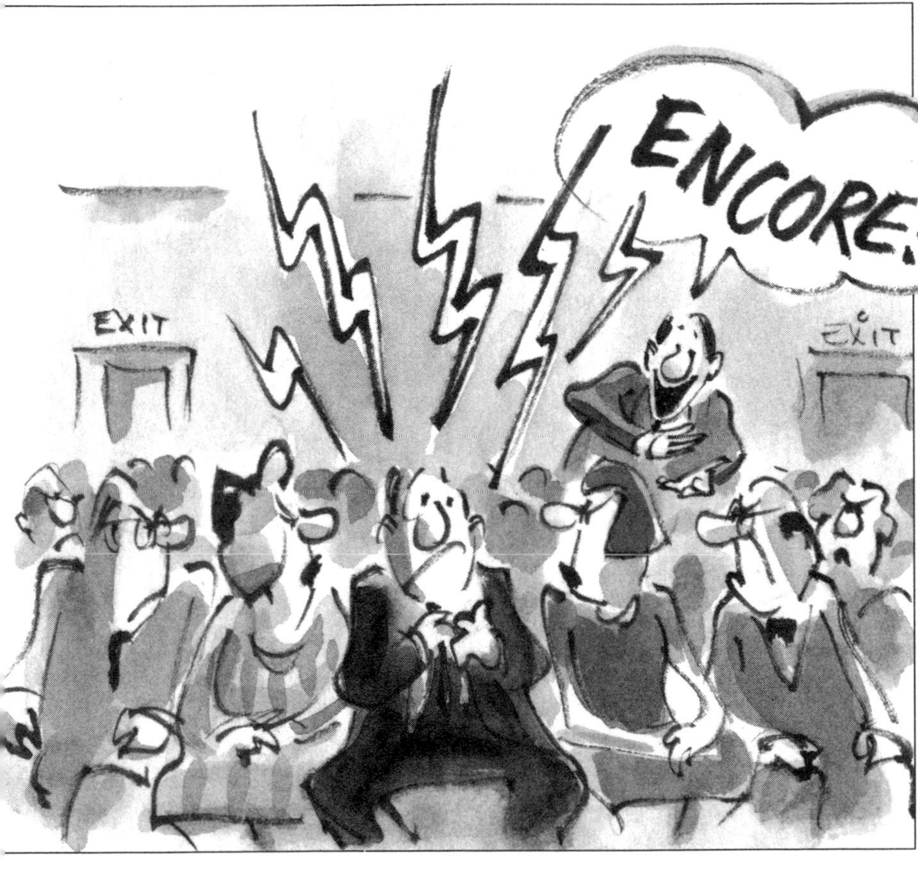

EXIT
ENCORE!
EXIT

You Know You're a Workaholic When. . .

You do at least three of the following while talking to friends on the phone:

vacuum
pay bills
brush teeth
cook dinner
eat dinner
wash the dishes
blow-dry your hair
bathe the dog
do your taxes
read magazines
listen to books on tape
go to sleep

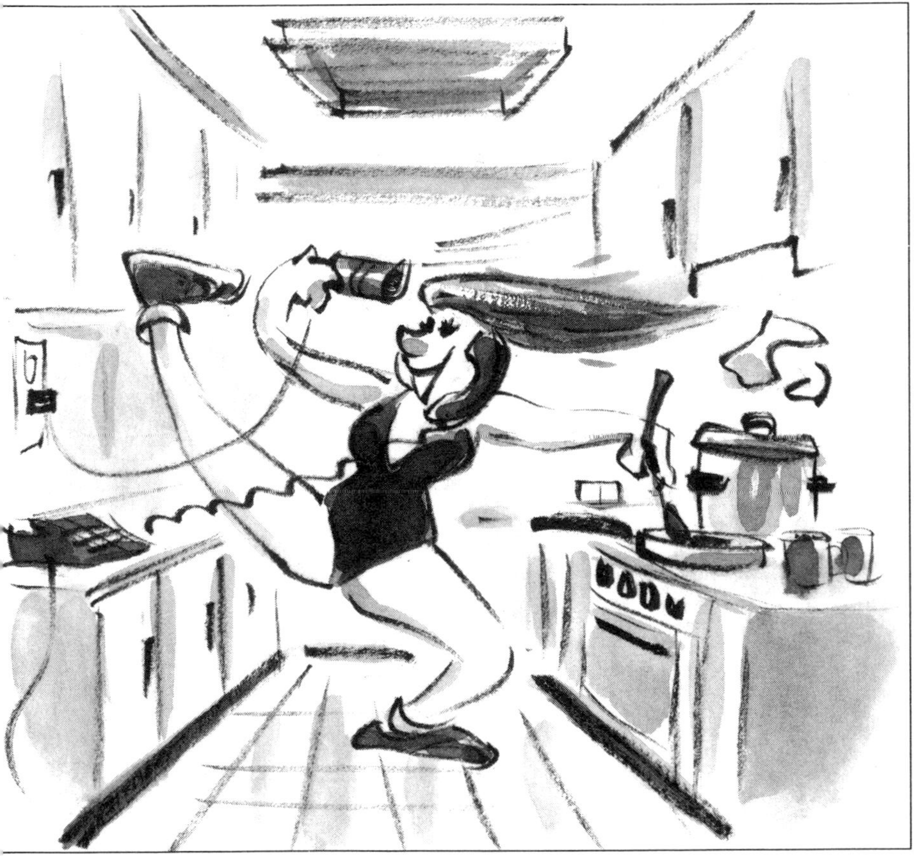

You Know You're a Workaholic When...

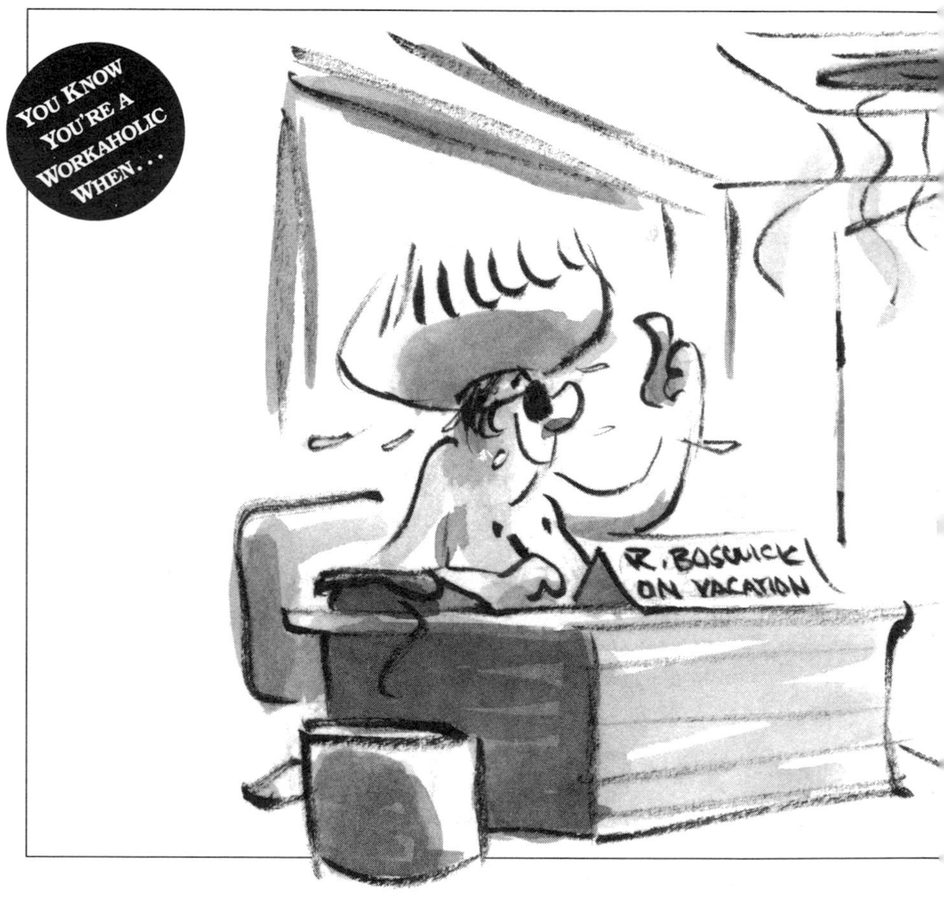
R. BOSWICK
ON VACATION

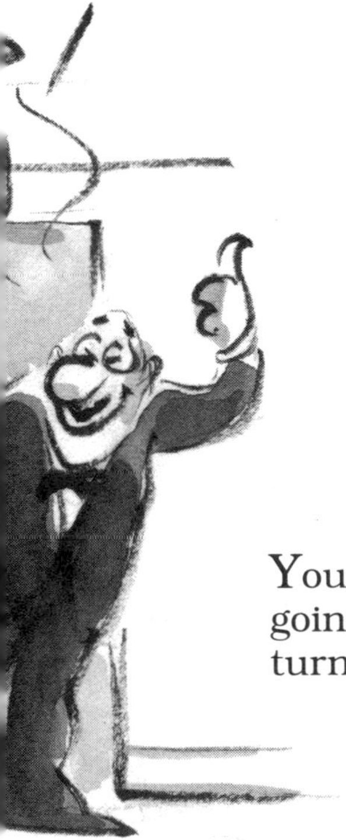

You tell your spouse that instead of going to the Caribbean, you'll simply turn up the heat in the office.

You Know You're a Workaholic When...

You'd never have an extramarital
affair because it would
cut into office hours.

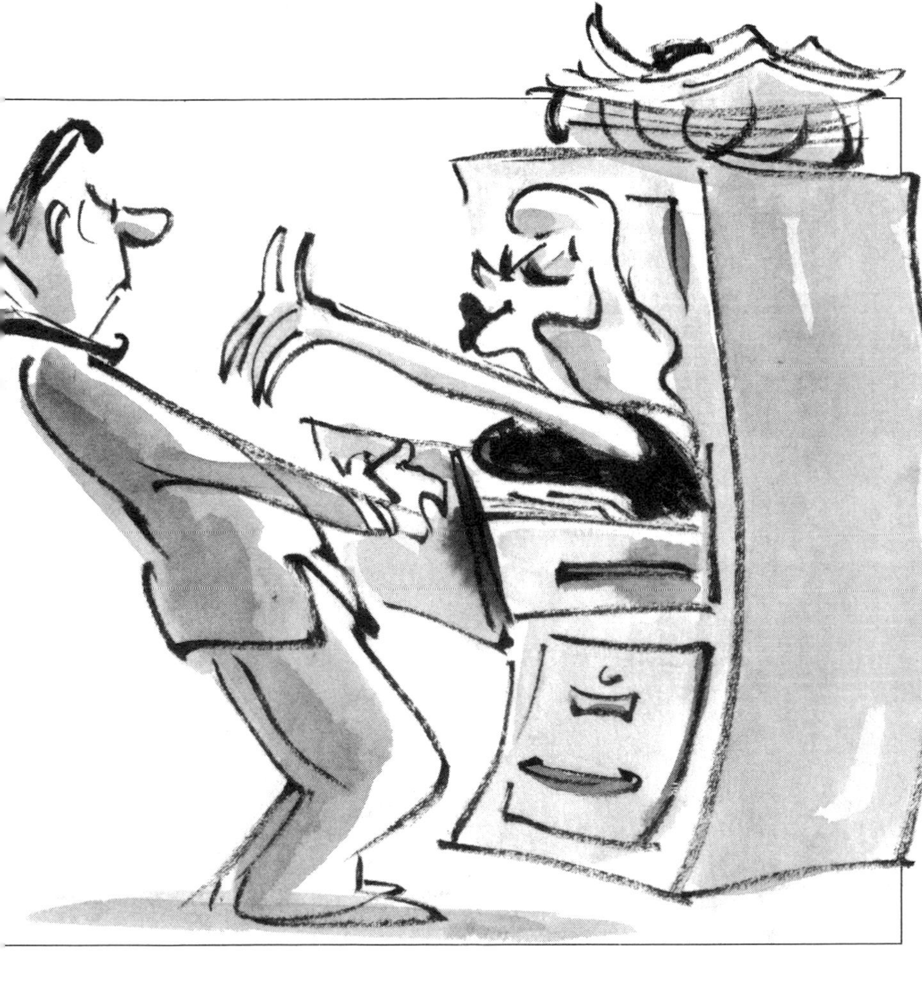

YOU KNOW YOU'RE A WORKAHOLIC WHEN...

You tie up all the phones at once in the airport telephone bank.

You can't understand why anyone would complain about insomnia.

You've never figured out the point of drying dishes.

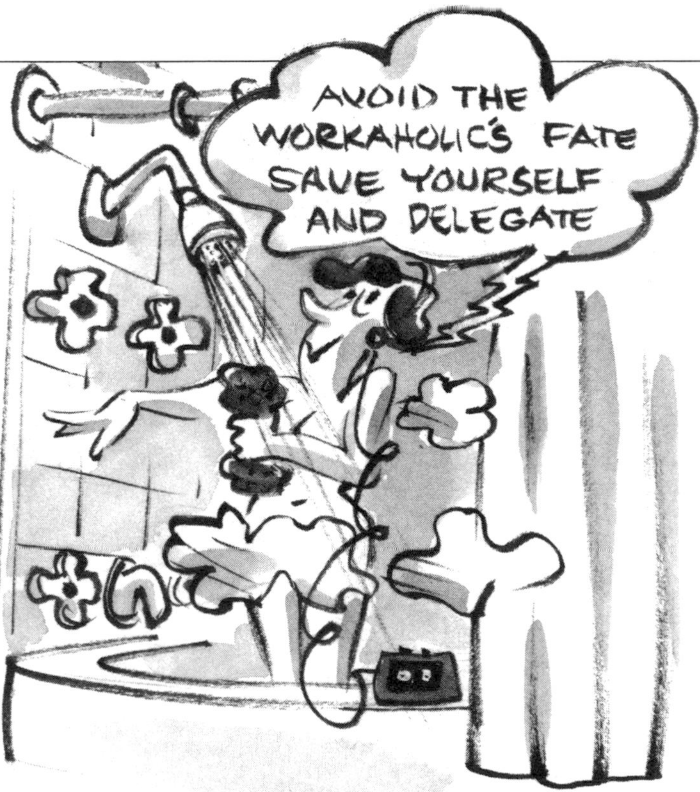
AVOID THE WORKAHOLIC'S FATE SAVE YOURSELF AND DELEGATE

You don't understand why everyone doesn't listen to management tapes in the shower.

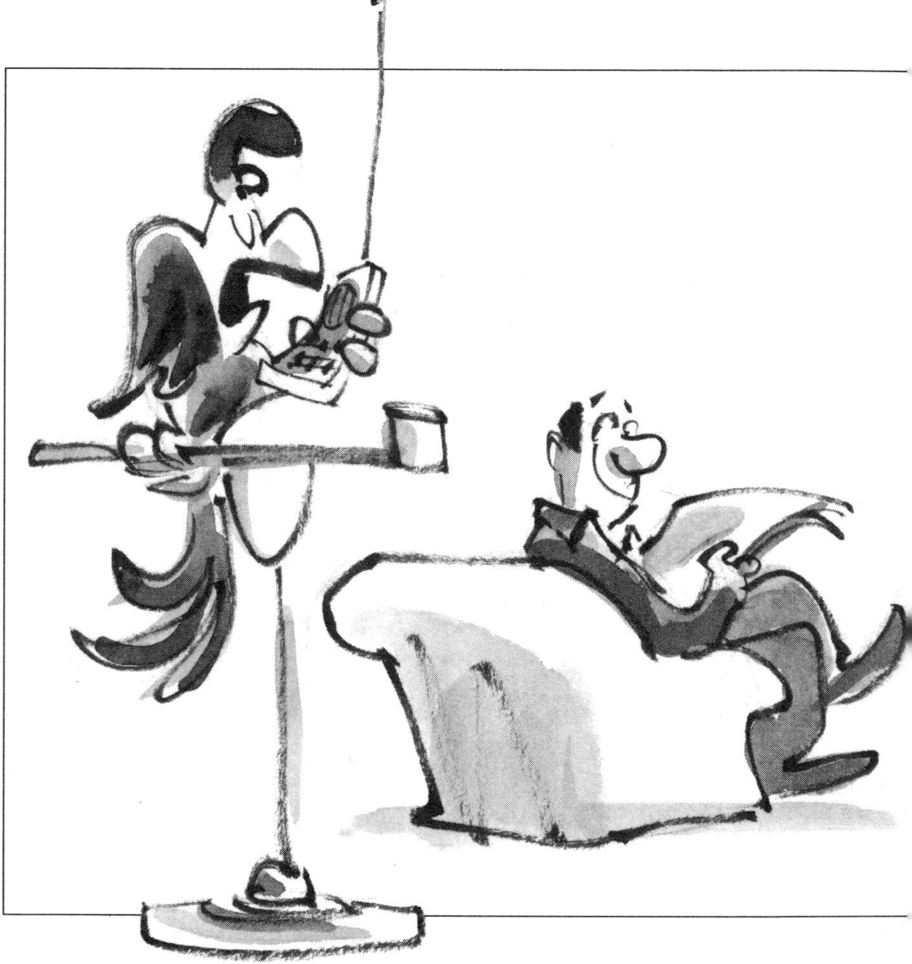

YOU KNOW YOU'RE A WORKAHOLIC WHEN...

Your parrot says, "Let's do lunch; Polly want a cracker."

You Know You're a Workaholic When...

You hate waiting for:

the elevator
Monday
the copy machine to warm up
your toddler to button his coat
your computer to save
the stock market to open
the waiter to finish reciting the specials
REM sleep

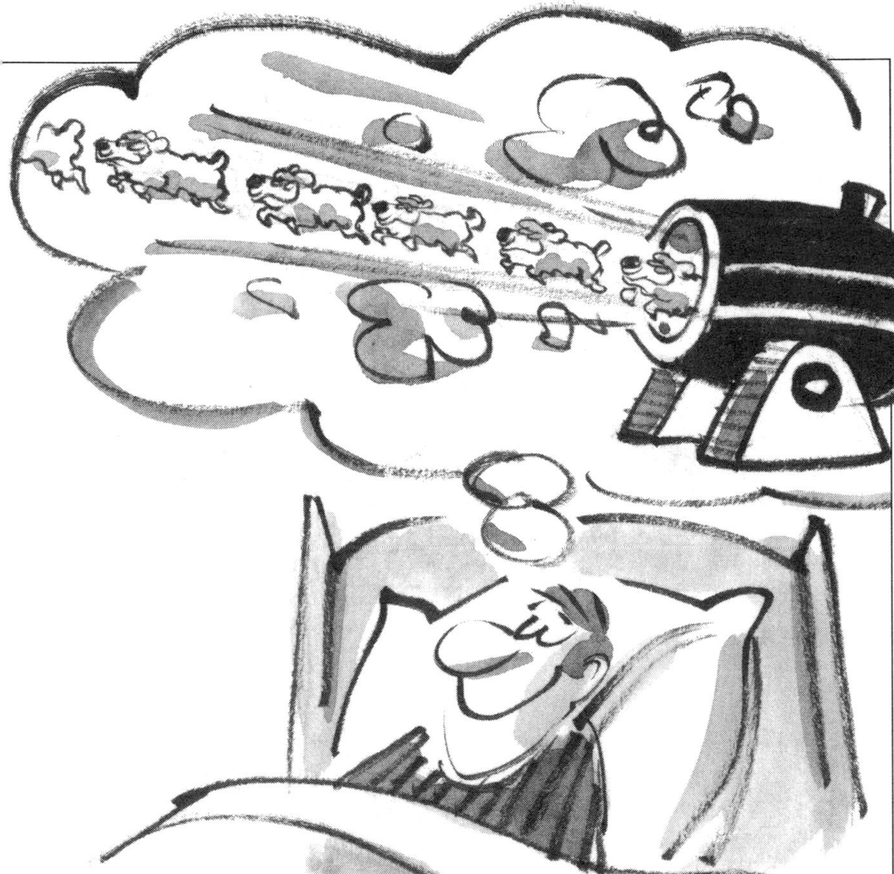

YOU KNOW YOU'RE A WORKAHOLIC WHEN. . .

You have a statue in your office of the man who stayed up 54 consecutive days.

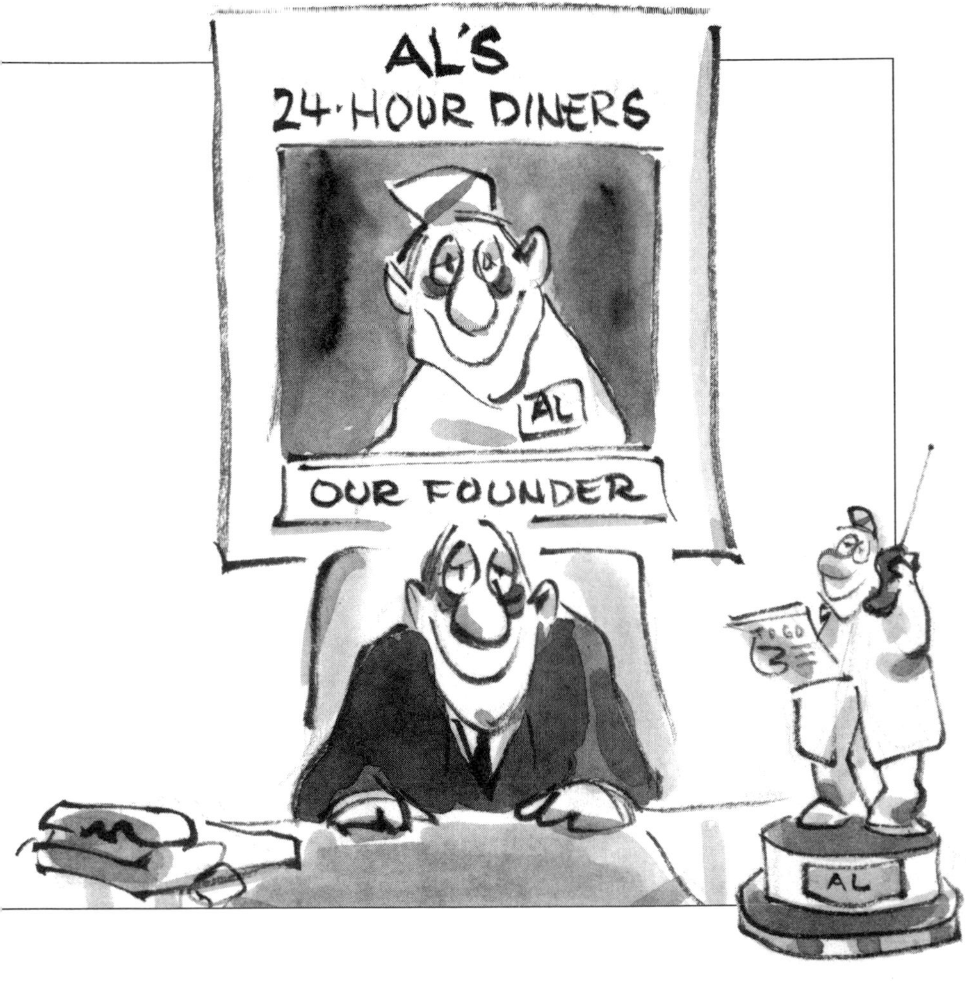
AL'S
24-HOUR DINERS
AL
OUR FOUNDER
AL

You Know You're a Workaholic When...

Your most meaningful relationship is with Mr. Coffee.

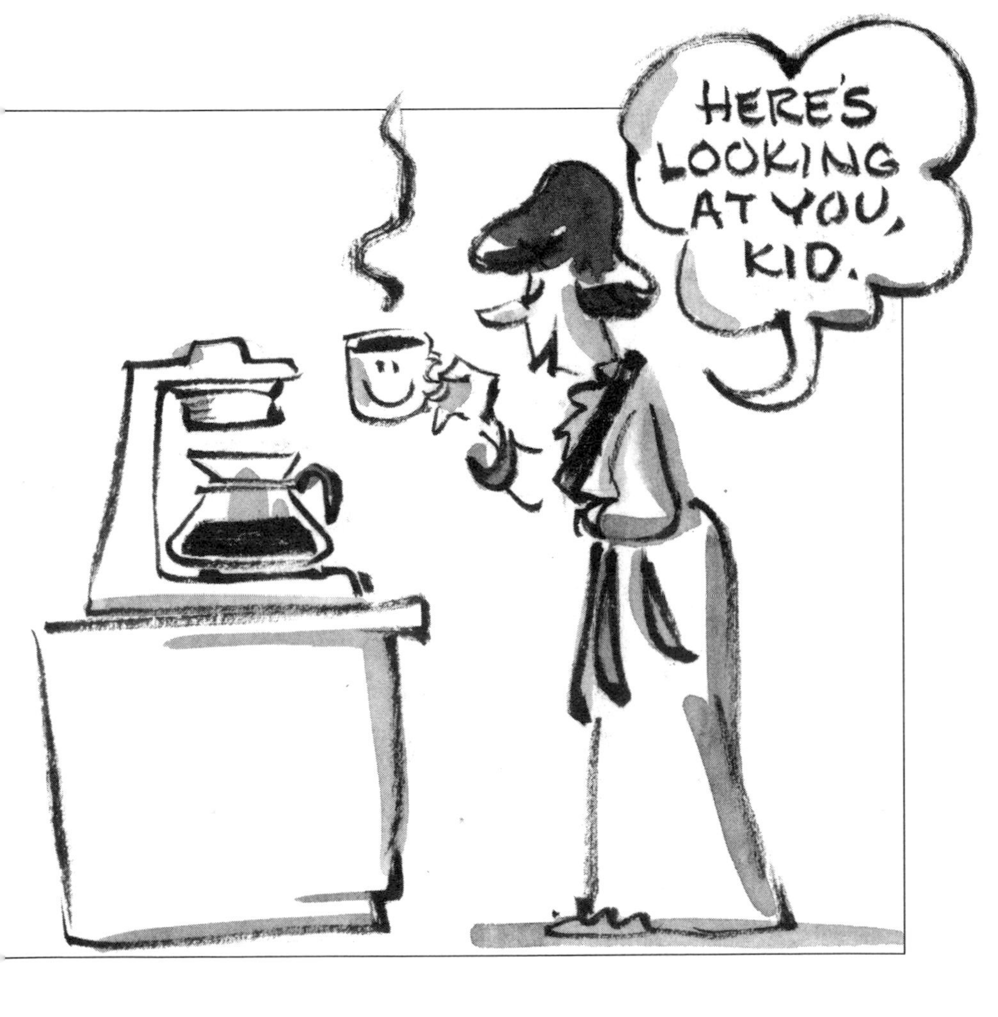
HERE'S LOOKING AT YOU, KID.

YOU KNOW YOU'RE A WORKAHOLIC WHEN...

You're in the habit of buying underwear and socks every week because Bloomingdale's stays open later than the laundry.

You feel guilty that you don't have carpal tunnel syndrome.

Your boss fires you but you organize his office birthday party anyway.

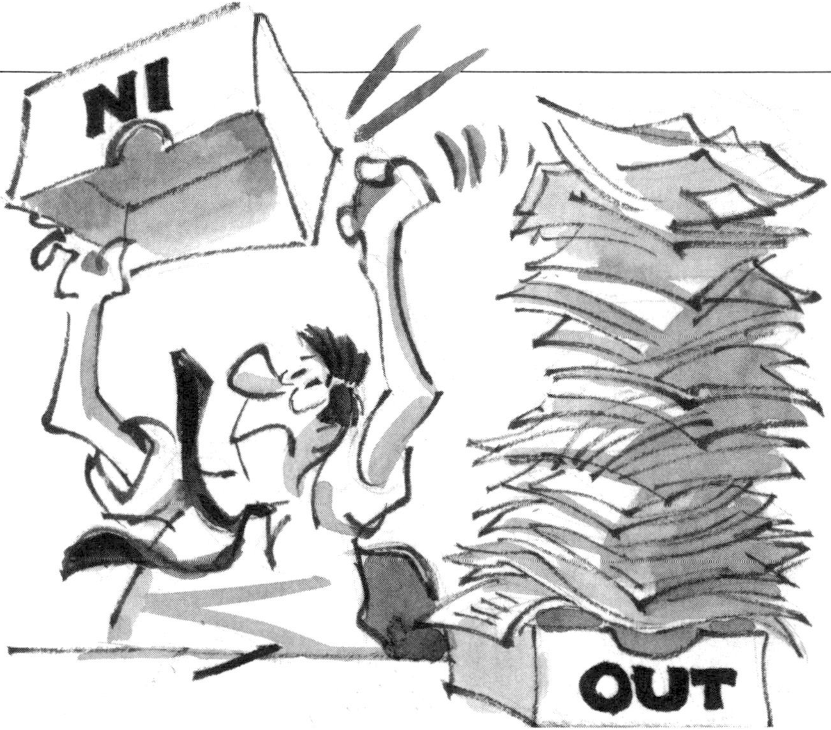
NI
OUT

You have an anxiety attack every time you finish a project.

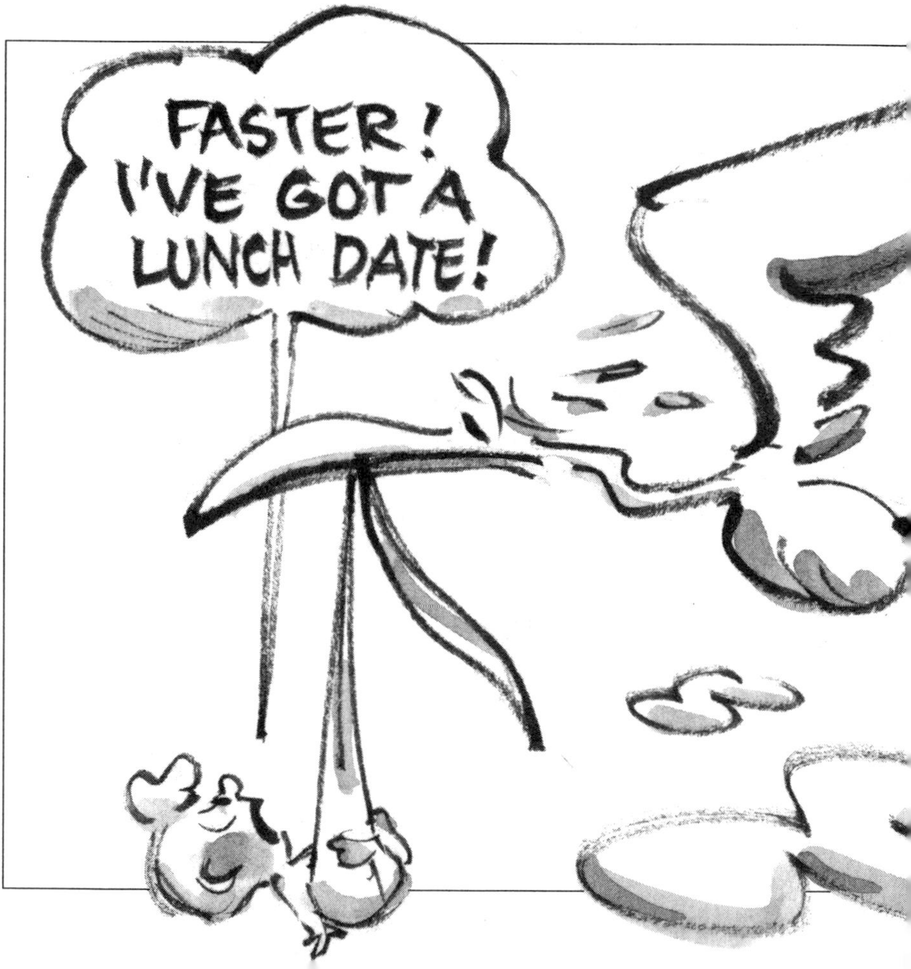
FASTER! I'VE GOT A LUNCH DATE!

YOU KNOW YOU'RE A WORKAHOLIC WHEN...

You'd love to have children . . .
but nine months seems like
an awfully long time to wait
for your heir apparent.

YOU KNOW YOU'RE A WORKAHOLIC WHEN...

The first eight numbers on your speed dialer are restaurants that deliver.

You wonder why certain hours are called "rush hours": isn't every hour rush hour?

You wonder how people can talk so slowly.

You think the bags under your eyes are sexy.

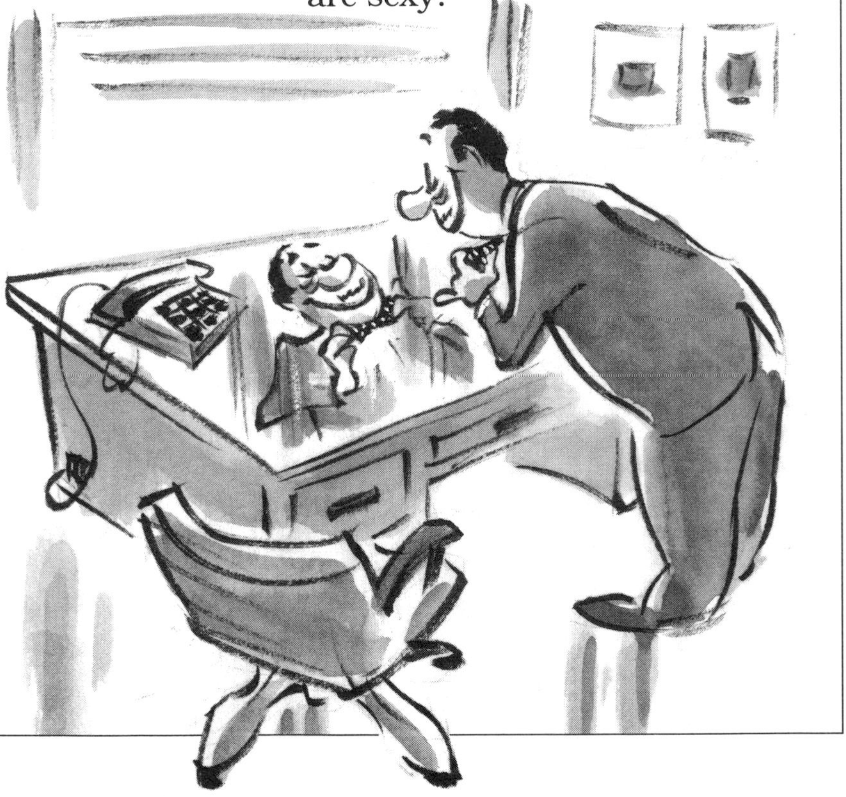

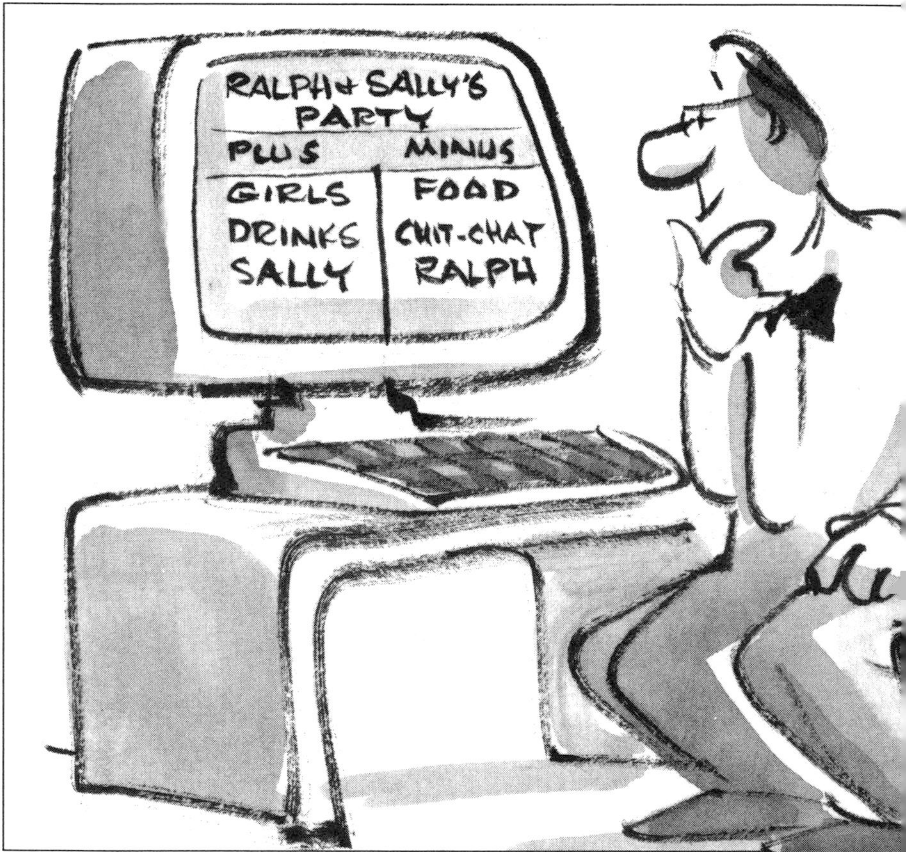
RALPH & SALLY'S PARTY
PLUS
MINUS
GIRLS
FOOD
DRINKS
CHIT-CHAT
SALLY
RALPH

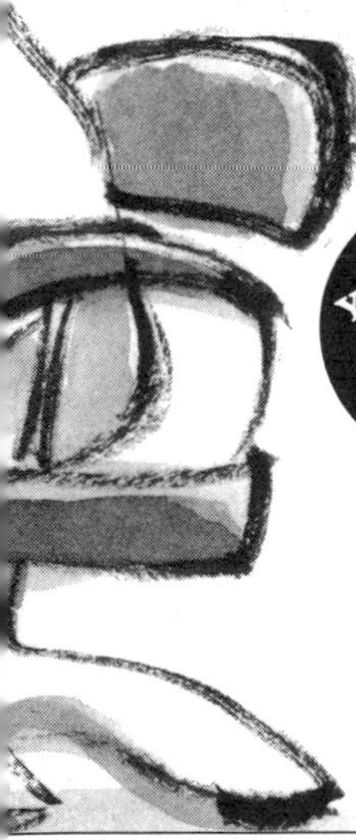

You Know You're a Workaholic When...

You consider the upside potential and downside risk before going to a party.

YOU KNOW YOU'RE A WORKAHOLIC WHEN...

You look at your watch at least:

2 times during sex
4 times as your father tells a joke
8 times during a movie
16 times during the last 30 seconds of
    the Super Bowl
24 times while you wait for the potato
    to bake in the microwave

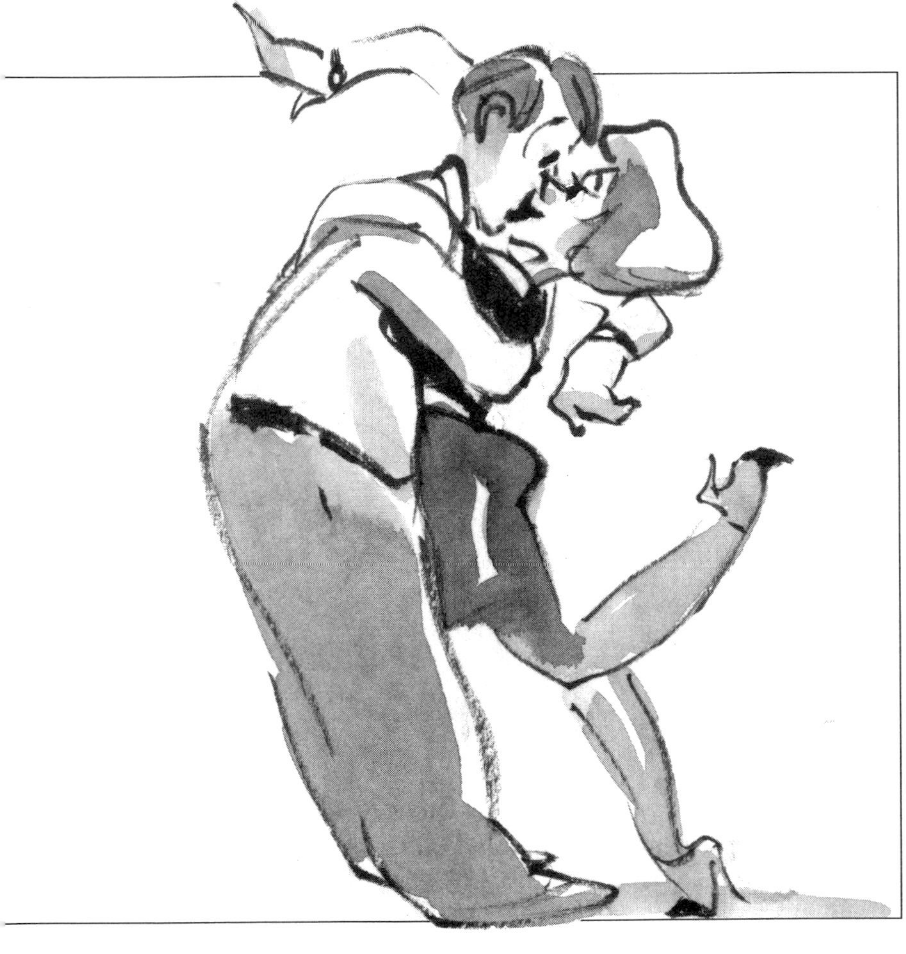

You Know You're a Workaholic When. . .

You see a psychiatrist to help you kick your doodling habit.

You've actually used up pencils before losing them.

You're nostalgic about homework.

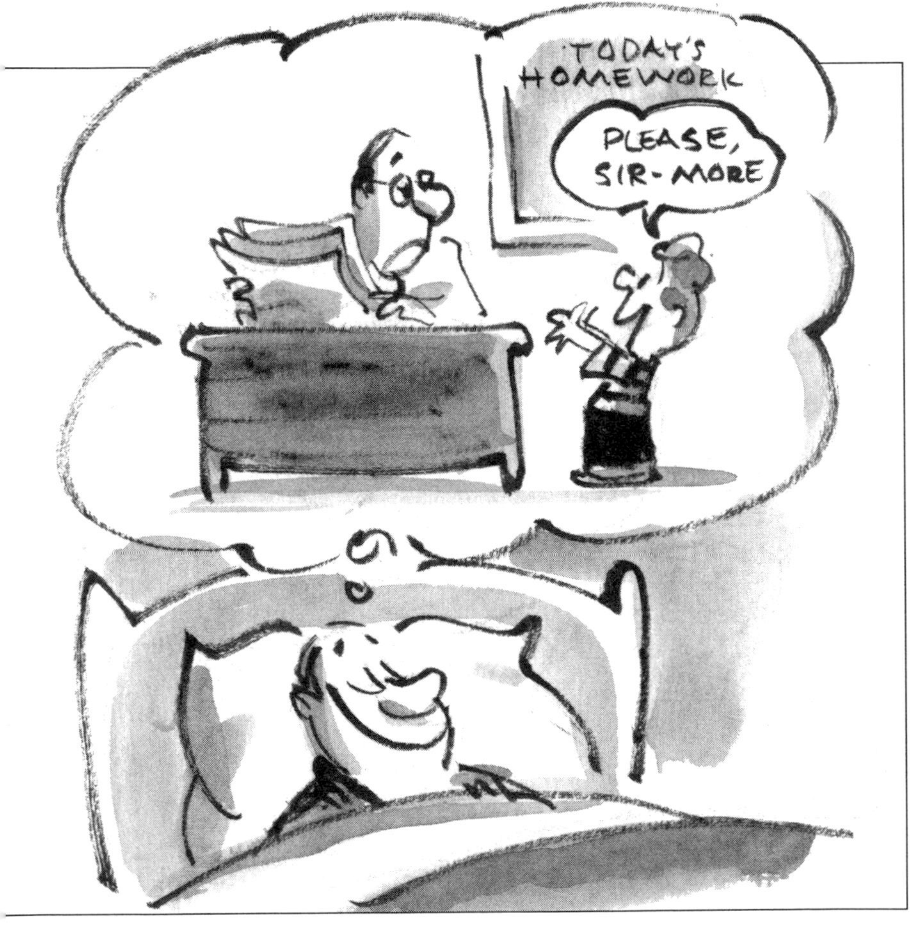
TODAY'S HOMEWORK
PLEASE, SIR - MORE

YOU KNOW YOU'RE A WORKAHOLIC WHEN...

You ignore the fire alarm so you can catch up on your call-backs.

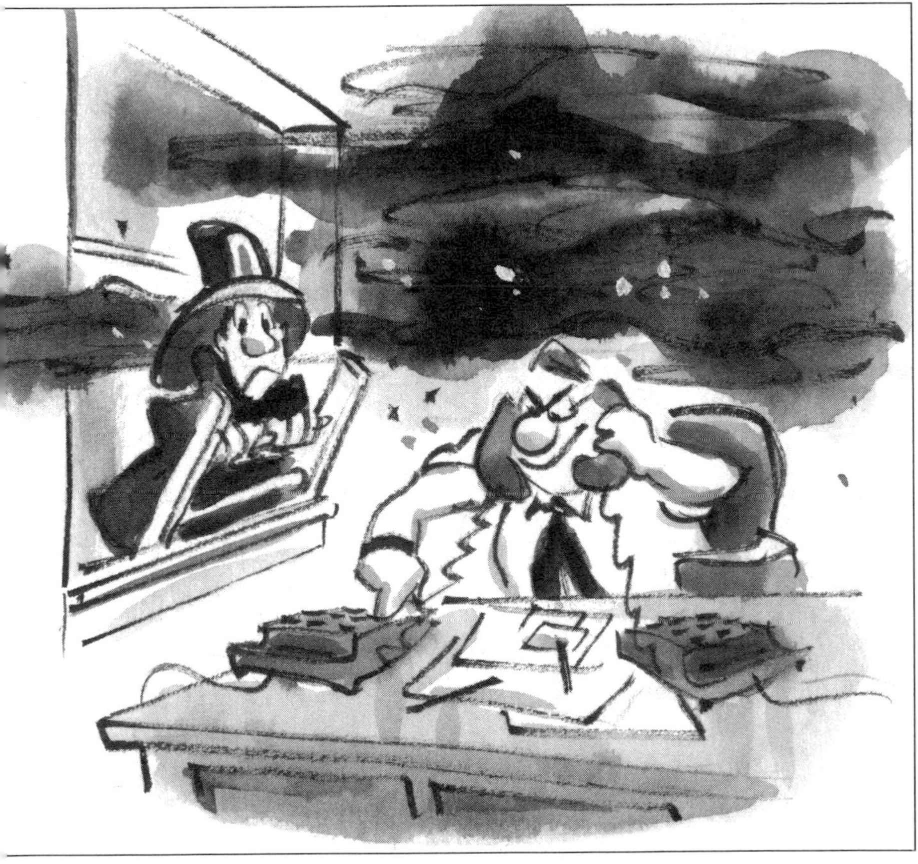

You Know You're A Workaholic When...

You think your office memos would make a good mini-series.

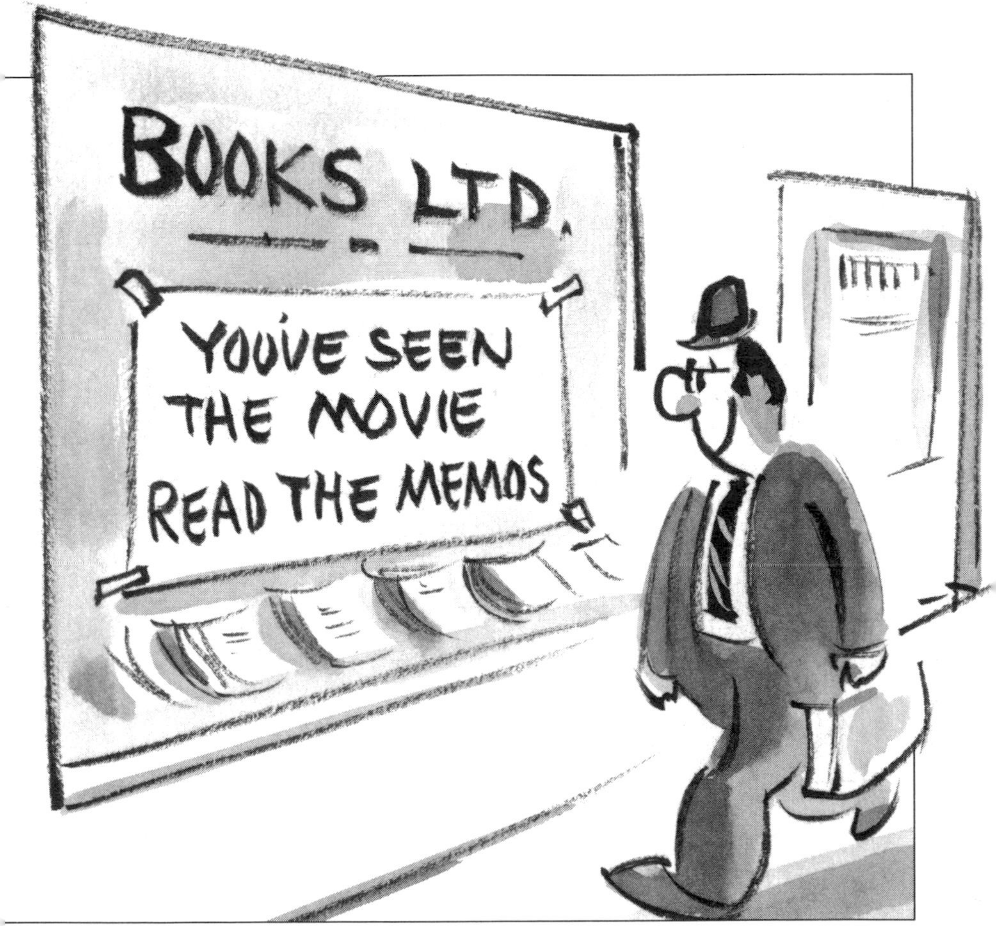
BOOKS LTD.
YOU'VE SEEN THE MOVIE
READ THE MEMOS

YOU KNOW YOU'RE A WORKAHOLIC WHEN...

You think people don't do enough business at business lunches.

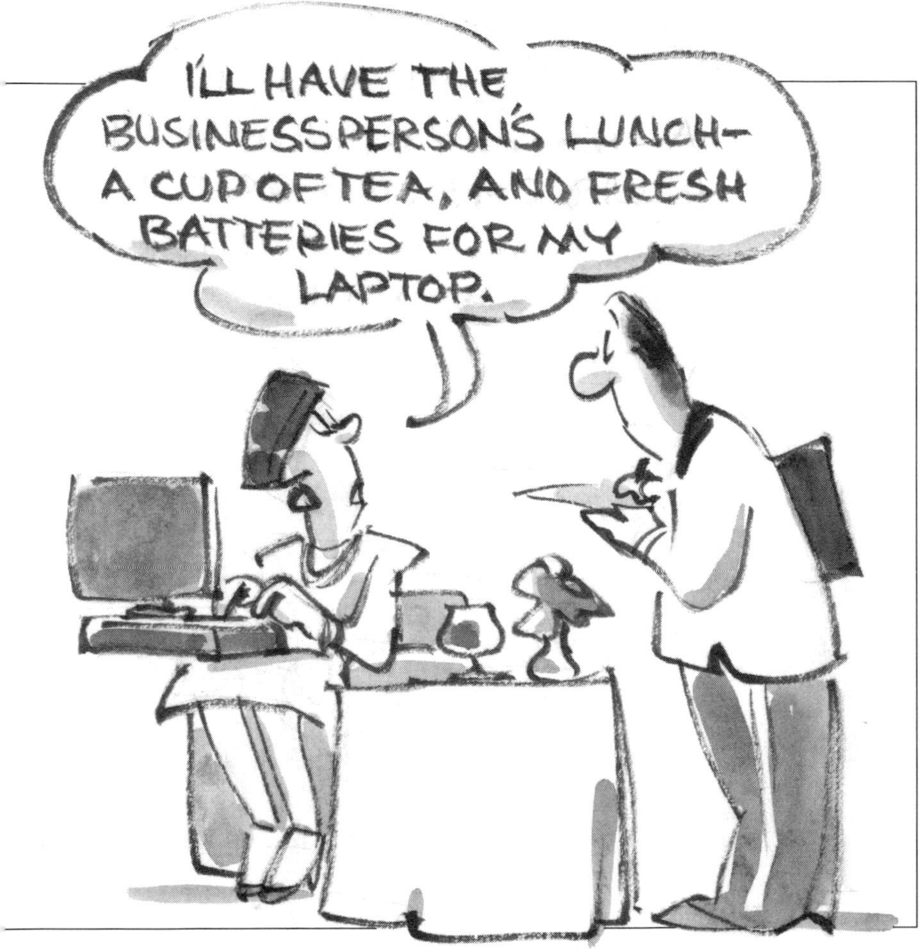
I'LL HAVE THE BUSINESSPERSON'S LUNCH- A CUP OF TEA, AND FRESH BATTERIES FOR MY LAPTOP.

YOU KNOW YOU'RE A WORKAHOLIC WHEN. . .

Your photo album is on microfiche.

You carry snapshots of your new copy machine.

You never go out with anyone whose resumé you haven't read.

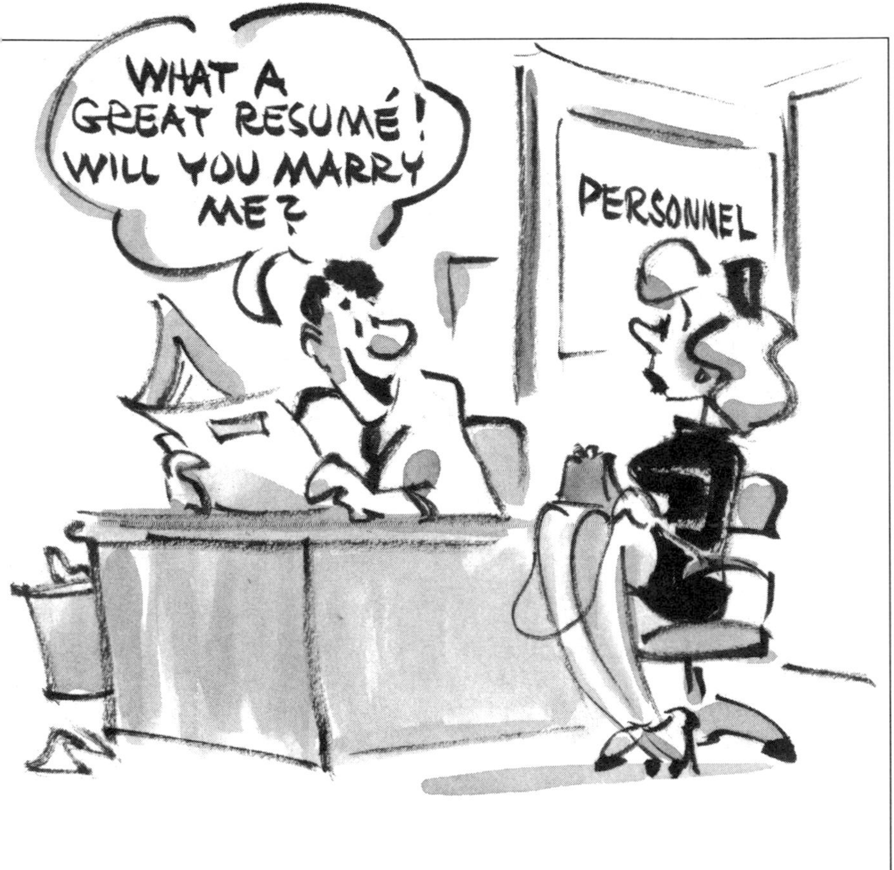
WHAT A GREAT RESUMÉ! WILL YOU MARRY ME?
PERSONNEL

YOU KNOW YOU'RE A WORKAHOLIC WHEN...

You wish everyone would use your extended zi
code so you could get your mail faste

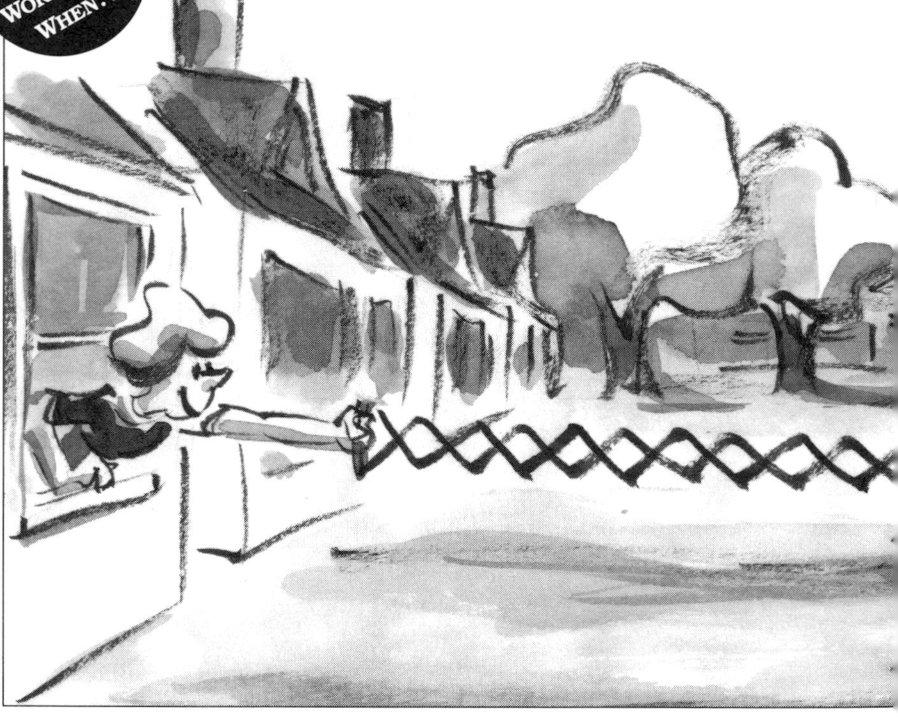

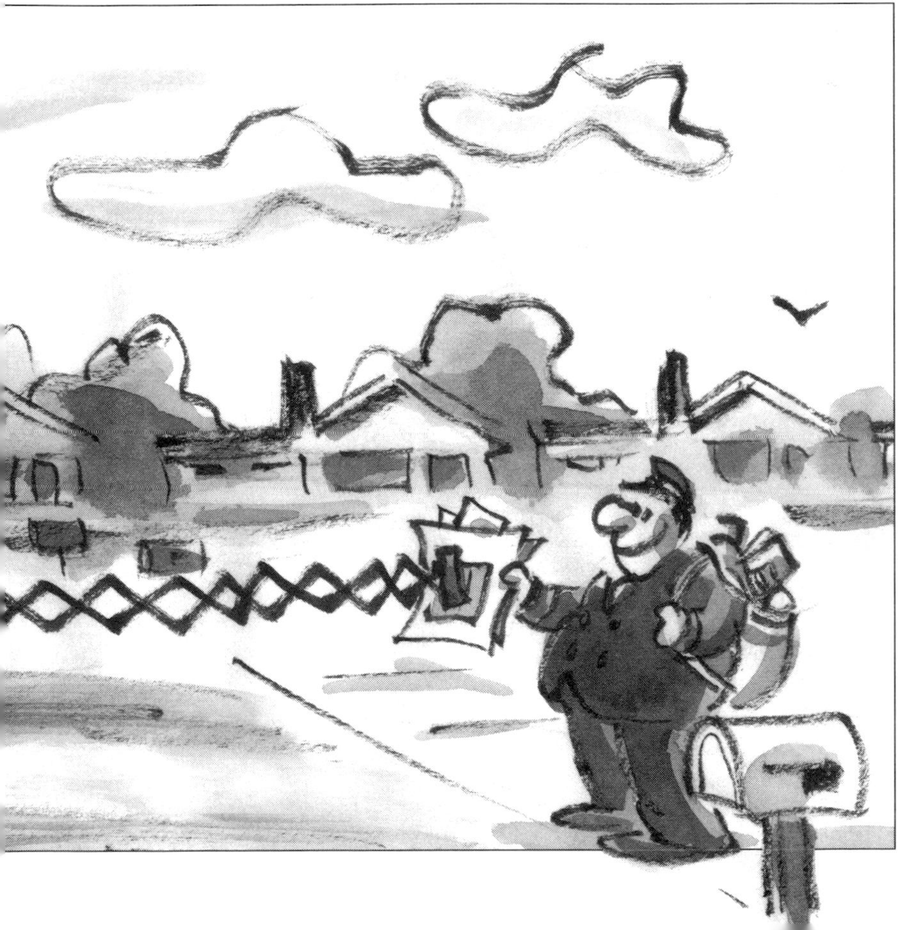

You Know You're a Workaholic When . . .

The psychiatrist shows you a Rorschach inkblot, and you either:

—tell him it looks like an oil spill caused by someone not paying attention to his job, or
—wonder why the painter didn't take the time to finish up the ragged edges, or
—think of all the time it will take someone to clean up the mess, or
—ask him if it's a new kind of graph, or
—say, "Well, that's what happens when you doodle with a fountain pen."

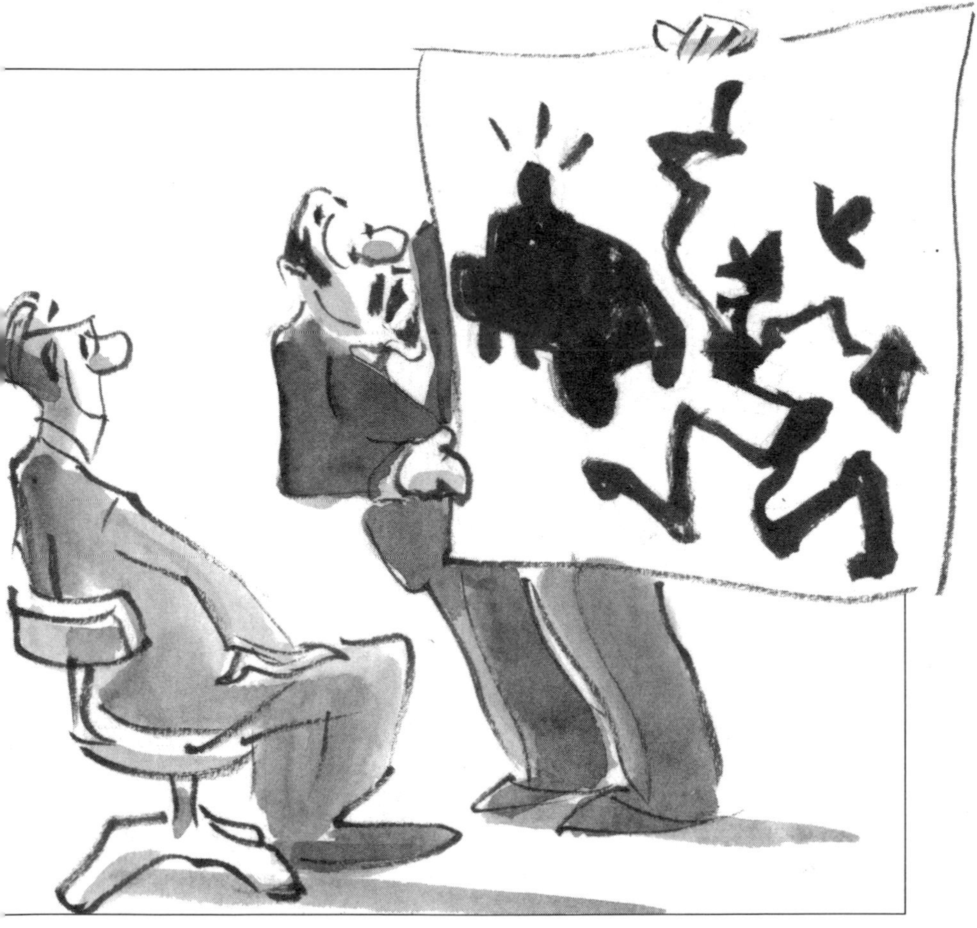

YOU KNOW YOU'RE A WORKAHOLIC WHEN . . .

You think people who do only two things at once are lazy.

You like to make lists of your lists.

You tell the dentist to skip the novocaine: "Root canal or no root canal, I've got a management seminar at noon!"

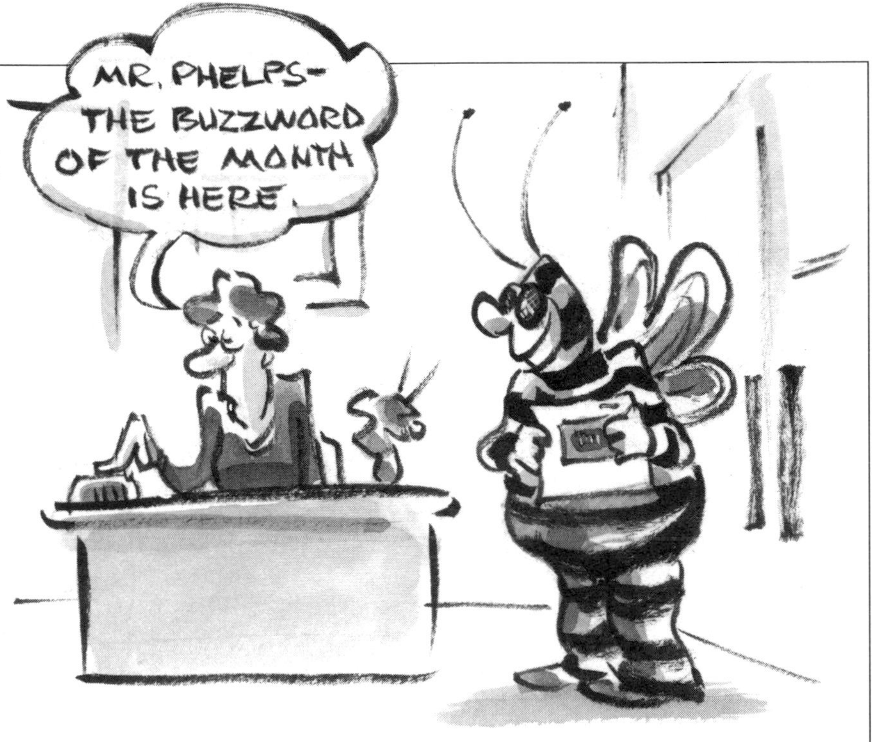
MR. PHELPS-
THE BUZZWORD
OF THE MONTH
IS HERE.

You subscribe to the fruit-of-the-month club, steak-of-the-month club and shampoo-of-the-month club so that you never have to shop.

YOU KNOW
YOU'RE A
WORKAHOLIC
WHEN...

You always stop at red lights . . . so you can shave or put on makeup, comb your hair, get dressed, eat and fax.

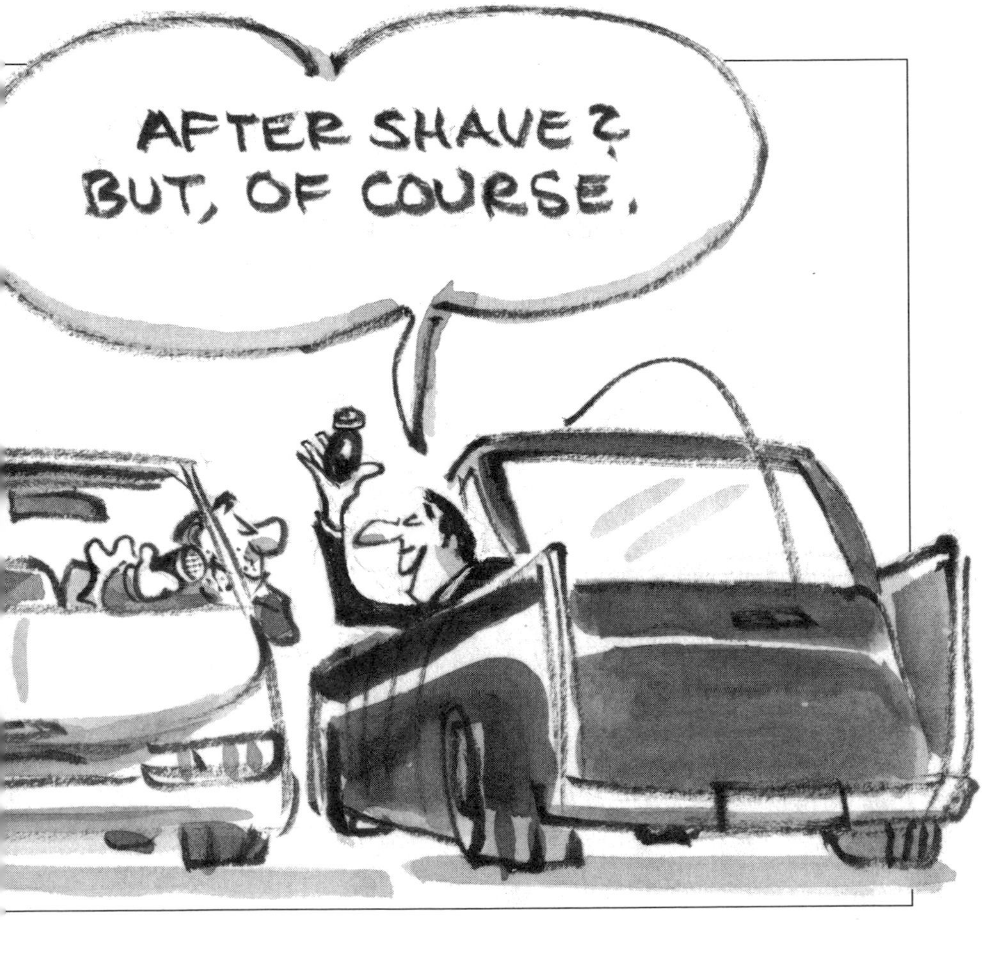
AFTER SHAVE? BUT, OF COURSE.

YOU KNOW YOU'RE A WORKAHOLIC WHEN...

You think a little less of God for resting on the seventh day.

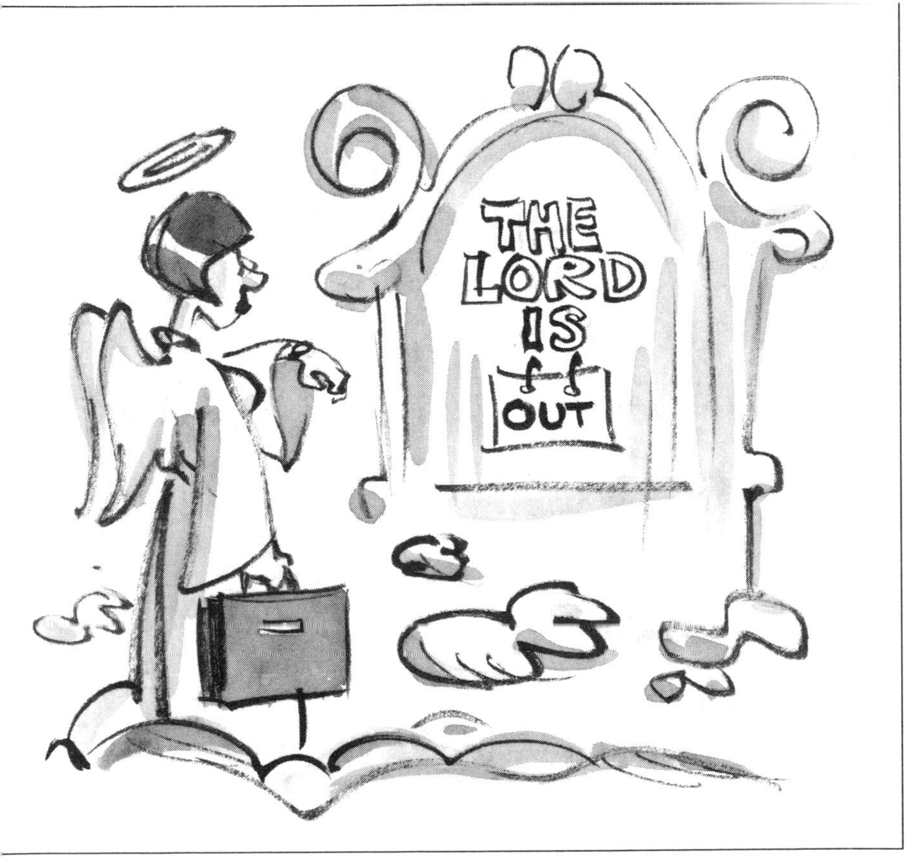
THE LORD IS
OUT

YOU KNOW YOU'RE A WORKAHOLIC WHEN...

You think all work and no play makes Jack a swell guy.

You weren't invited to the office party because you remind everyone of work.

You think of an ulcer as a badge of courage.

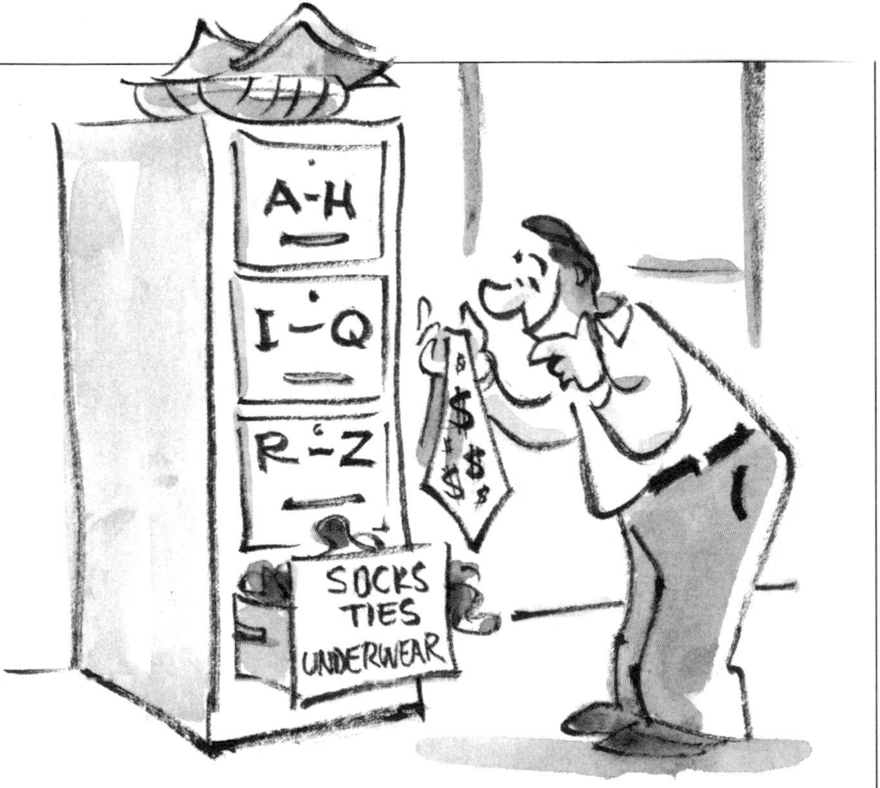
A-H
I-Q
R-Z
SOCKS
TIES
UNDERWEAR

There are more clothes in your
desk drawer than in your bedroom closet.

You Know You're a Workaholic When...

You've heard a lot about the weather but you've never actually seen it.

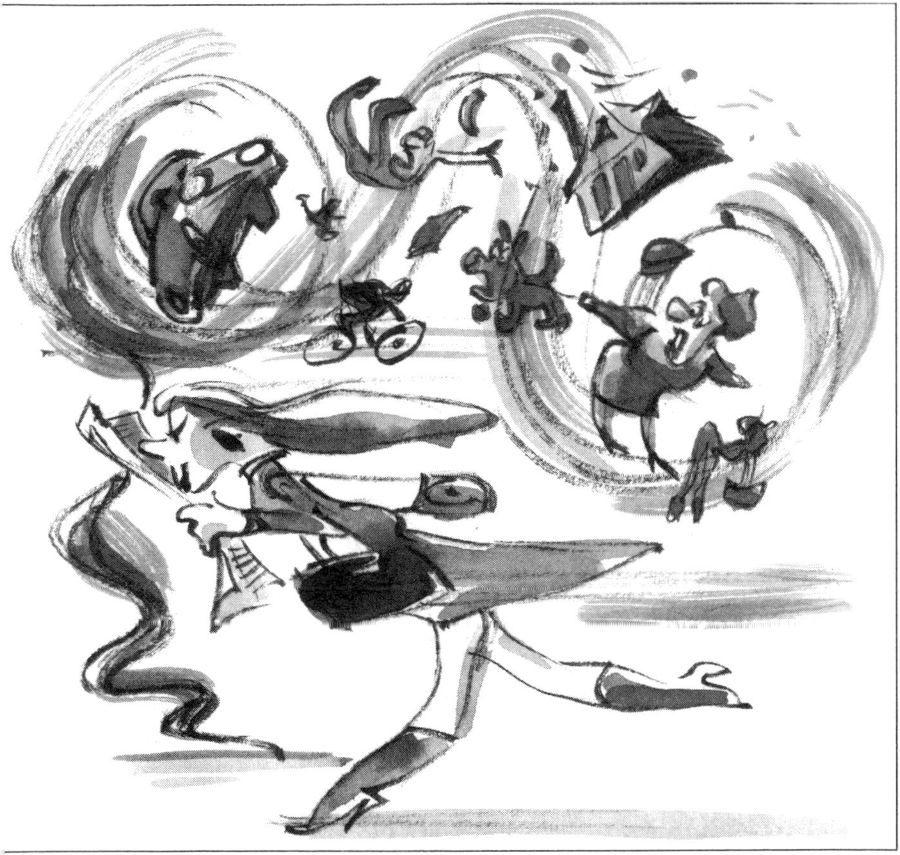

You Know You're a Workaholic When. . .

Someone gives you a book on chair aerobics.

You use scotch tape to fix your hems and jumbo paper clips to keep your hair out of your eyes.

There simply aren't enough billable hours in the day.

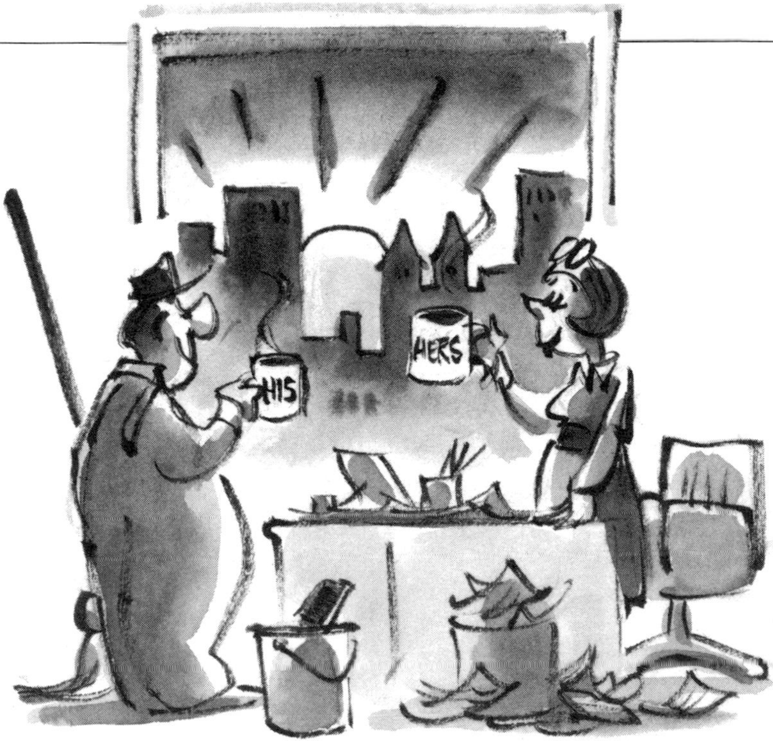
HIS
HERS

You've seen the sun rise more times with the late-night custodian than with your spouse.

YOU KNOW YOU'RE A WORKAHOLIC WHEN...

Hearing from your office always makes your day.

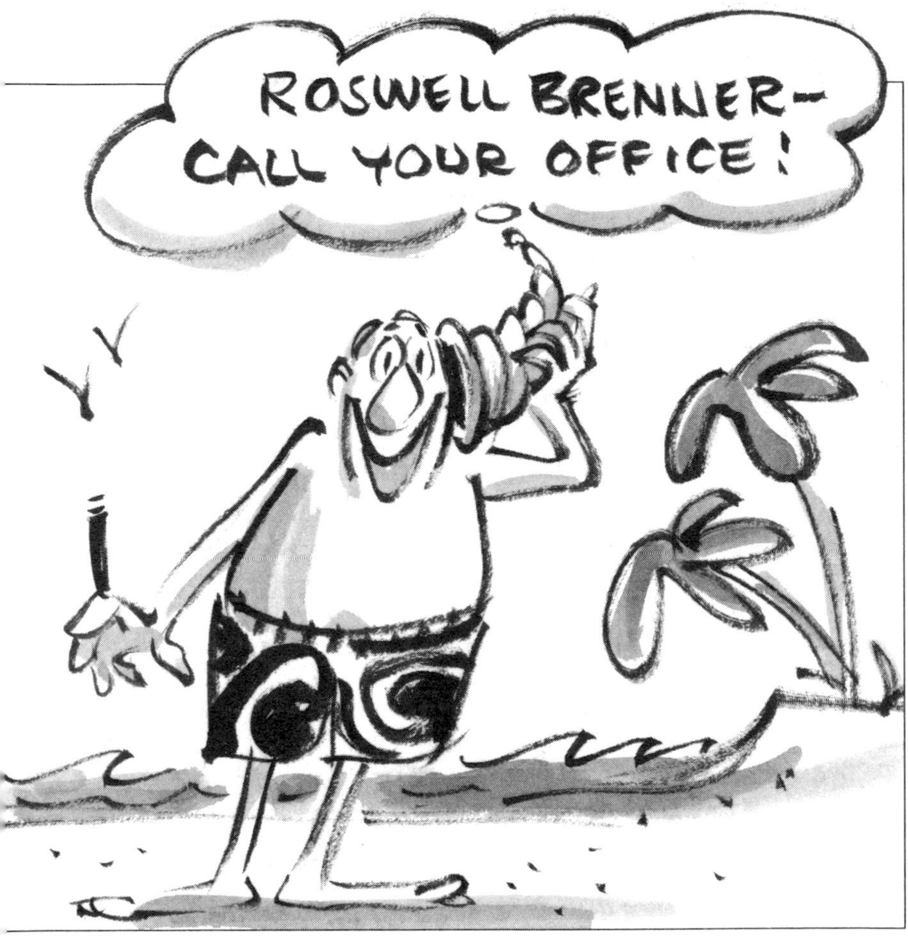
ROSWELL BRENNER–
CALL YOUR OFFICE!

YOU KNOW YOU'RE A WORKAHOLIC WHEN. . .

You order your corporate Christmas gifts in August (the same day you get your calendar for the following year).

You're sorry there were child labor laws when you were a kid.

Your children call you Mr. Daddy or Mrs. Mommy.

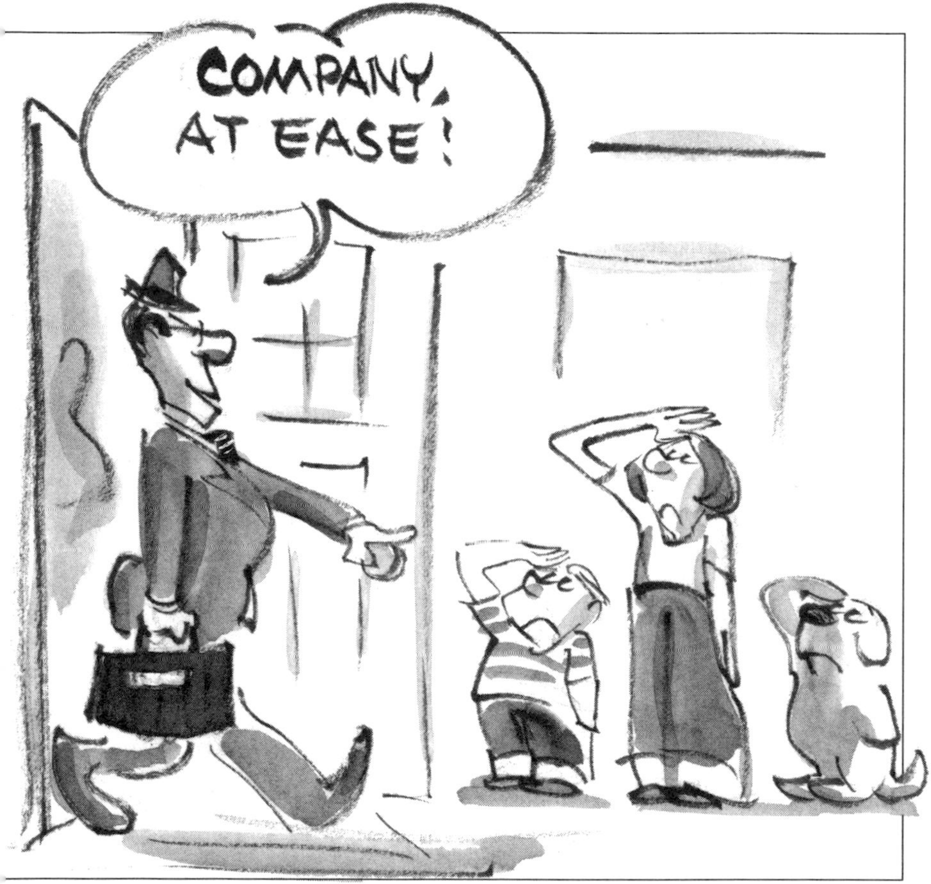
COMPANY, AT EASE!

YOU KNOW YOU'RE A WORKAHOLIC WHEN...

Your favorite foods include:

Carnation Instant Breakfast
Nestlés Quik
Minute Rice
Jiffy Pop
Redi-Whip

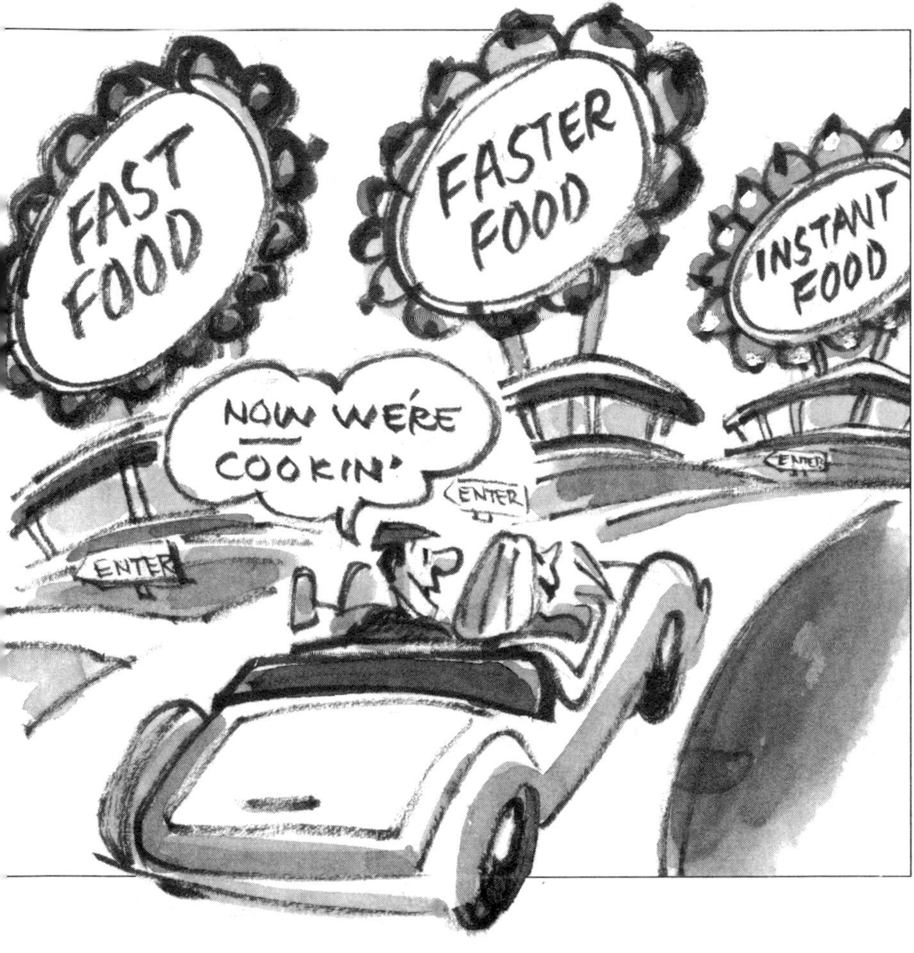
FAST FOOD
FASTER FOOD
INSTANT FOOD
NOW WE'RE COOKIN'
ENTER
ENTER
ENTER

YOU KNOW YOU'RE A WORKAHOLIC WHEN . . .

You think that the best thing about nudist colonies is how time-efficient they are.

You prefer poems to novels because they're shorter.

You've cut your hair short to save time on grooming.

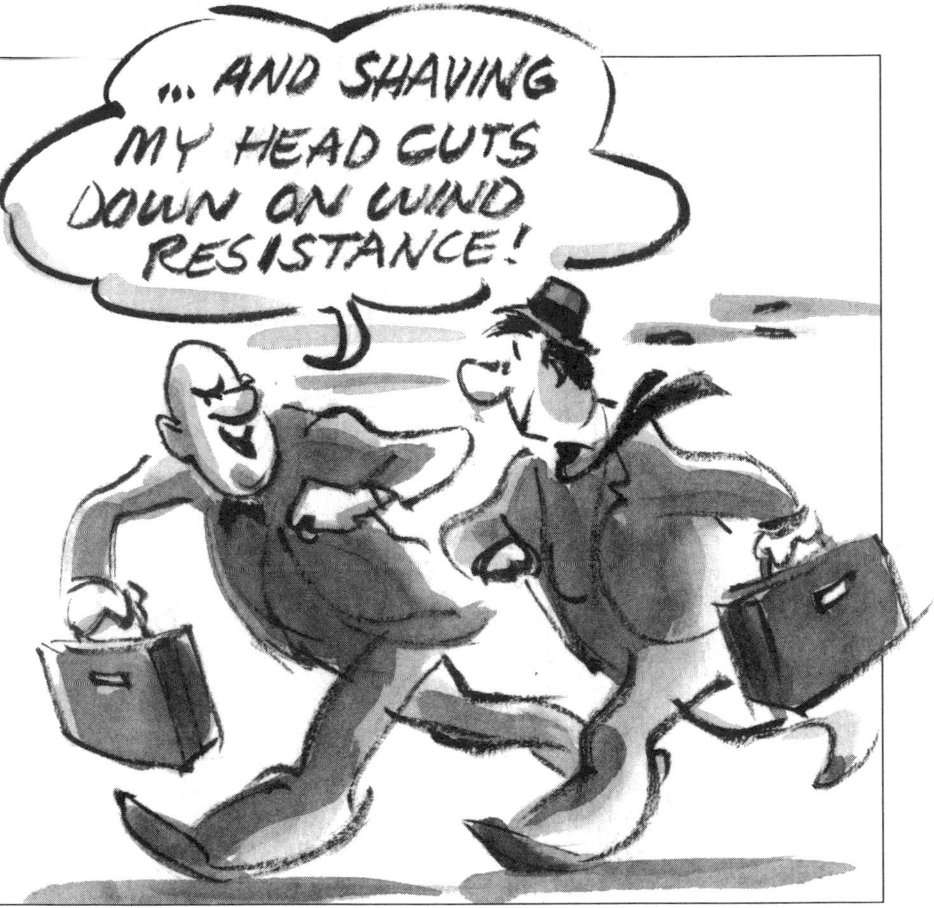
... AND SHAVING MY HEAD CUTS DOWN ON WIND RESISTANCE!

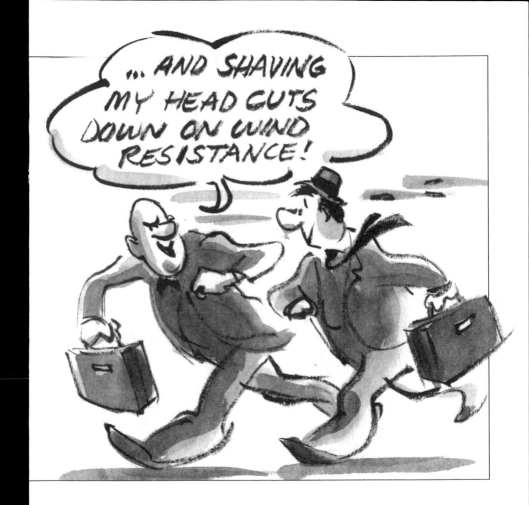

YOU KNOW YOU'RE A WORKAHOLIC WHEN. . .

You agree with Noël Coward that work is so much more fun than fun.

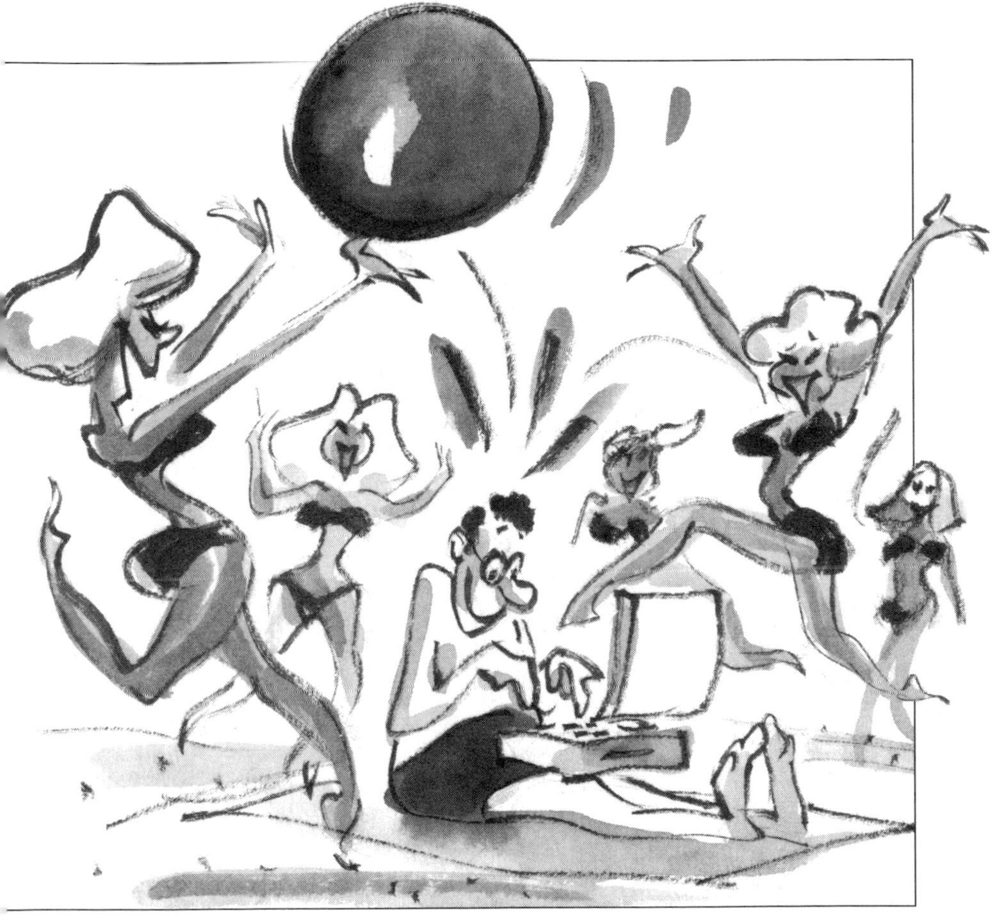

YOU KNOW YOU'RE A WORKAHOLIC WHEN. . .

You never go to restaurants that have music because it's too hard to hold a conversation on your cellular phone.

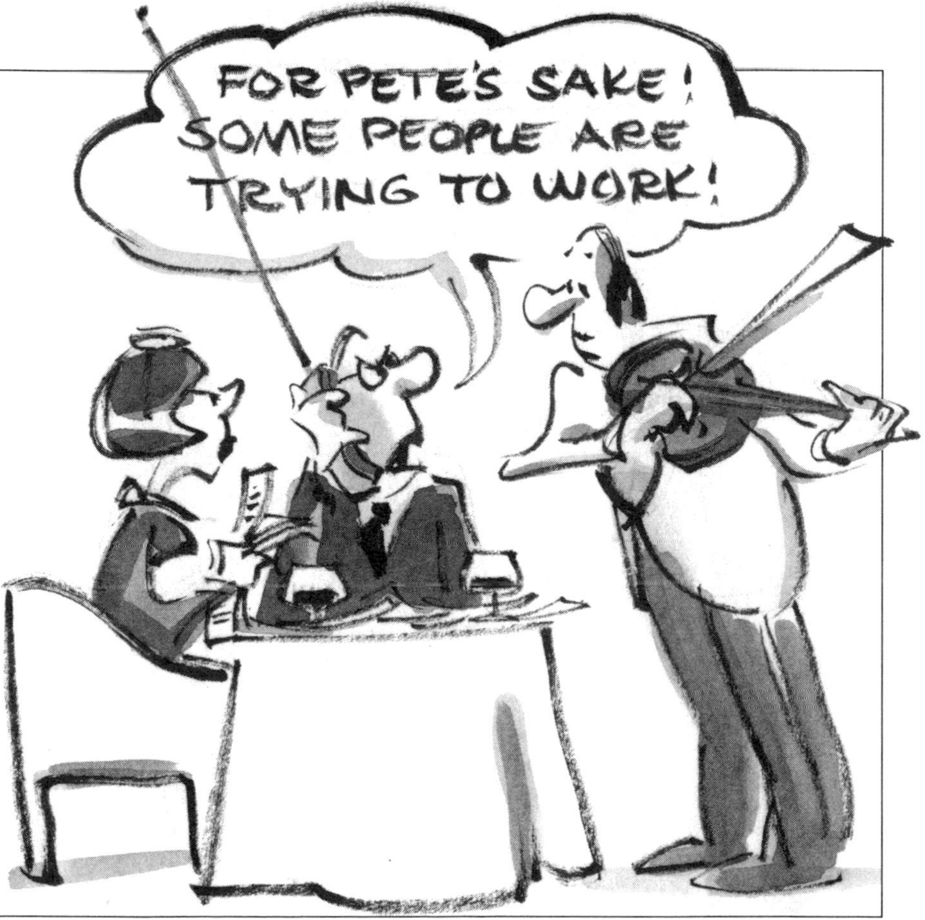
FOR PETE'S SAKE! SOME PEOPLE ARE TRYING TO WORK!

YOU KNOW YOU'RE A WORKAHOLIC WHEN...

You love Christmas because no one bothers you at the office.

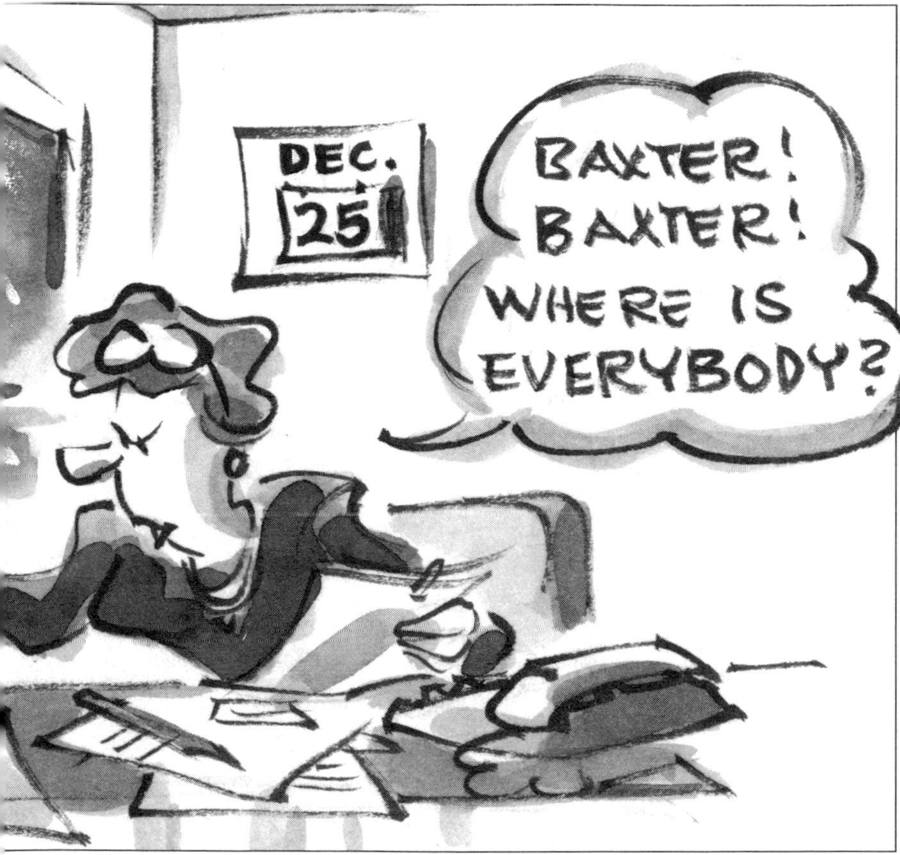
DEC.
25
BAXTER!
BAXTER!
WHERE IS
EVERYBODY?

You Know You're a Workaholic When. . . .

You present the minister with an annotated plan for paring down the moment of silence.

You think there's a market for home vending machines.

You dread the day in April when clocks are set forward.

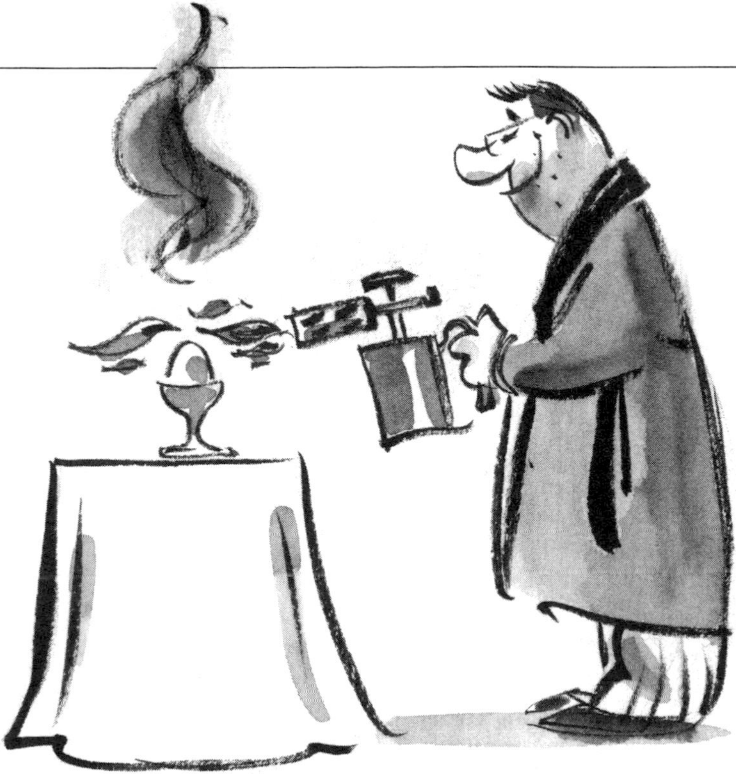

It takes you three minutes to boil a five-minute egg.

YOU KNOW YOU'RE A WORKAHOLIC WHEN...

You bring a flashlight to the theater so you can work on your marketing plan.

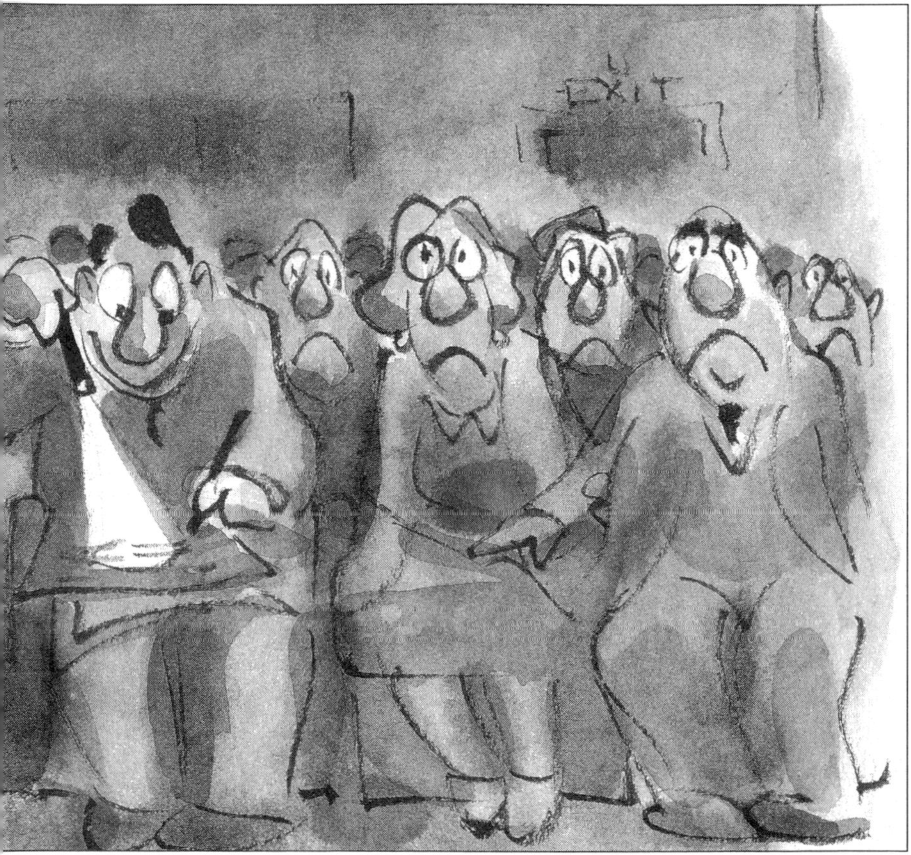
EXIT

You Know You're a Workaholic When . . .

You and the Federal Express man are on a first-name basis.

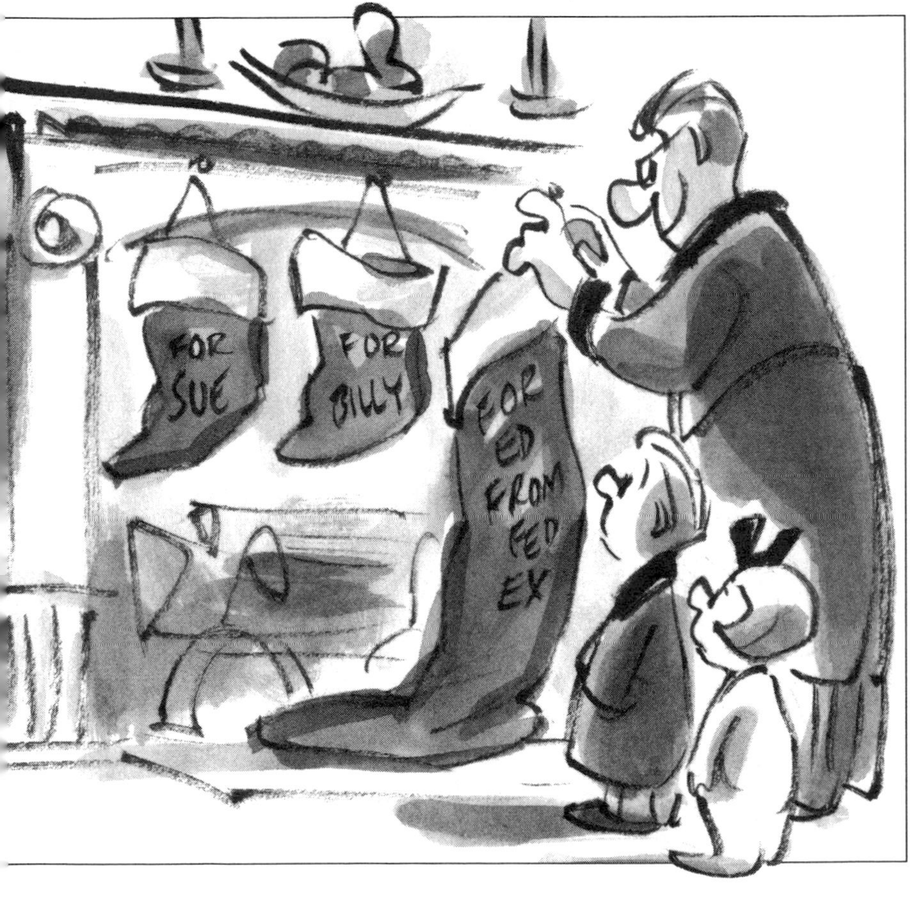
FOR SUE
FOR BILLY
FOR ED FROM FED EX

YOU KNOW YOU'RE A WORKAHOLIC WHEN...

Nobody, but nobody, knows how hard you work.

Your living will stipulates that the plug should be pulled if you ever become too sick to proofread your memos.

You will *never* retire.

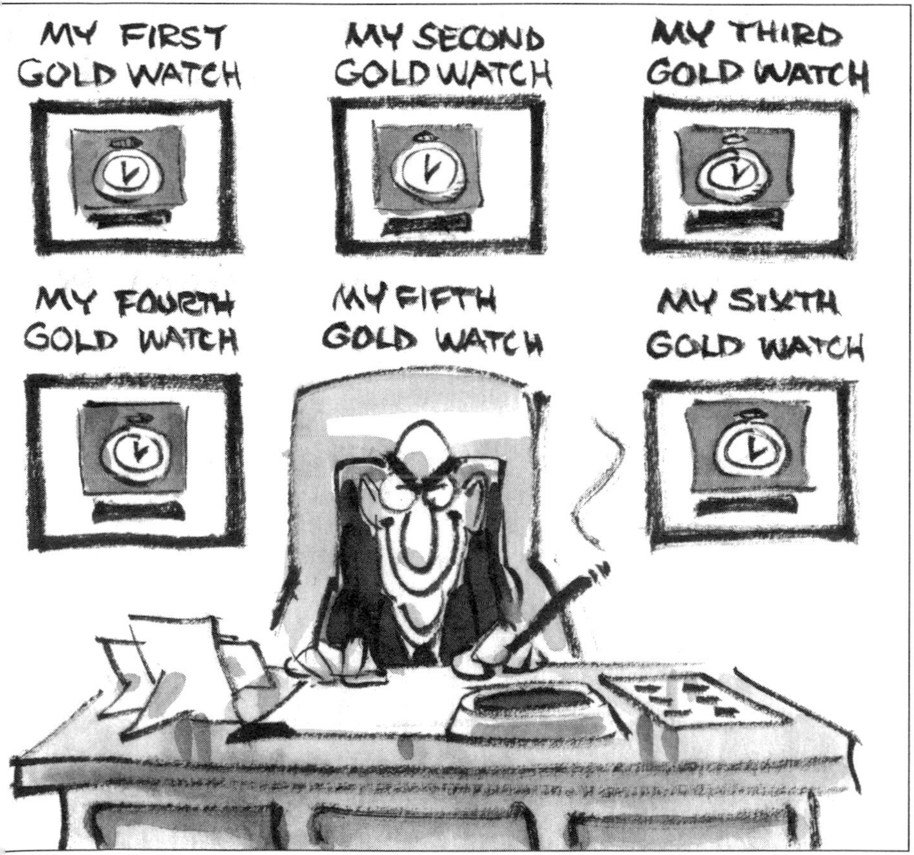
MY FIRST GOLD WATCH
MY SECOND GOLD WATCH
MY THIRD GOLD WATCH
MY FOURTH GOLD WATCH
MY FIFTH GOLD WATCH
MY SIXTH GOLD WATCH

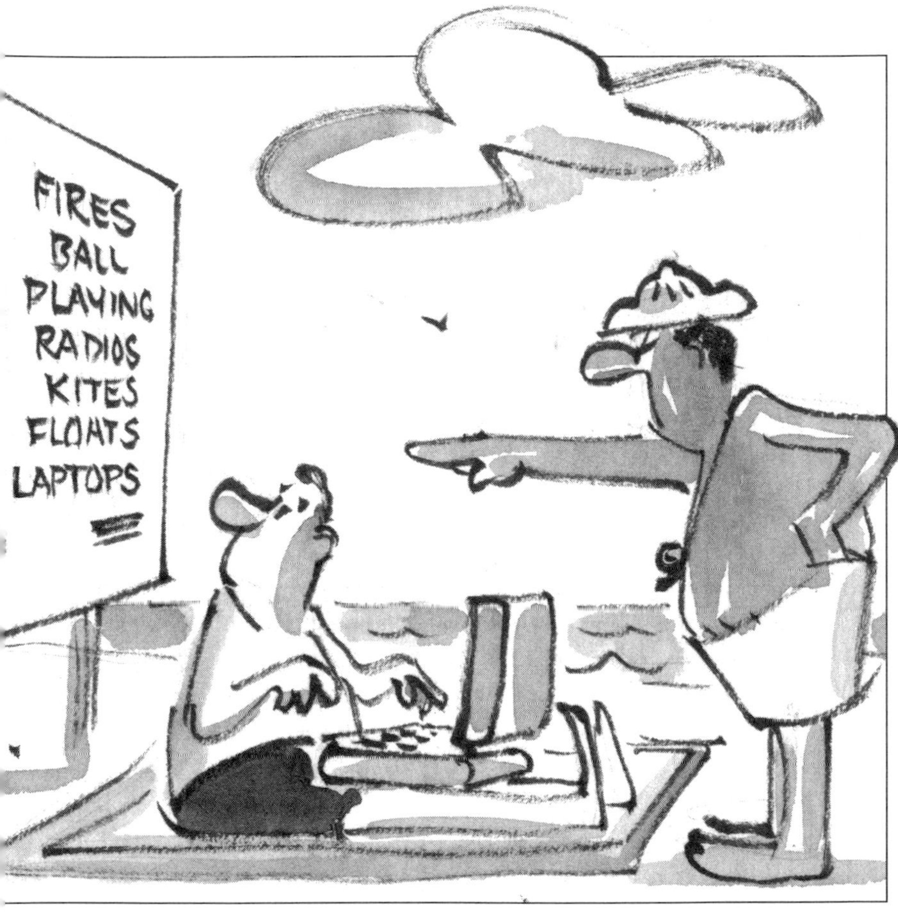
FIRES
BALL
PLAYING
RADIOS
KITES
FLOATS
LAPTOPS

You Know You're a Workaholic When...

Your comment, after seeing *Death of a Salesman*, is "too much broken hopes and dreams and not enough zero-base budgeting and total quality management."

The office supply store you patronize sends you flowers on your birthday.

Your idea of a great dinner conversationalist is a talking book.